Study Guide to Accompany
STATISTICS for the
BEHAVIORAL SCIENCES

FOURTH EDITION

FREDERICK J GRAVETTER

State University of New York
College at Brockport

LARRY B. WALLNAU

State University of New York
College at Brockport

WEST PUBLISHING COMPANY

Minneapolis/St. Paul/New York/Los Angeles/San Francisco

Production, Prepress, Printing and Binding by West Publishing Company.

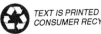
TEXT IS PRINTED ON 10% POST CONSUMER RECYCLED PAPER

COPYRIGHT © 1996 by WEST PUBLISHING CO.
610 Opperman Drive
P.O. Box 64526
St. Paul, MN 55164–0526

ISBN 0–314–06811–2

STUDY GUIDE TO ACCOMPANY
STATISTICS FOR THE BEHAVIORAL SCIENCES
(FOURTH EDITION)

CONTENTS

HOW TO USE
THIS STUDY GUIDE

As the title indicates, the purpose of a Study Guide is to provide you with a guide for studying. In general, studying involves revisiting and reviewing material that you have already seen in class and in the textbook. Notice that we have used the word "review," as in "a second look." The textbook is written to provide an introduction to statistical concepts, and includes all the explanations and examples necessary to present new ideas that students are seeing for the first time. This <u>Study Guide</u>, on the other hand, is written to provide a second look at material that is already somewhat familiar. That is, the Study Guide is intended as a "review" that condenses, summarizes, and highlights the textbook. Thus, the Study Guide is a supplement to the textbook, not a replacement for the textbook, and we strongly suggest that you work in the Study Guide only after you have read and studied the corresponding section in the textbook.

Each chapter in the Study Guide corresponds to a chapter in the textbook, and each Study Guide chapter is divided into seven major sections. The following paragraphs provide an overview of these sections and some suggestions for how they should be used.

Chapter Summary. We begin with a big-picture overview of the chapter contents. The intent is to provide a relatively concise summary of the general content of the chapter and to identify most of the major points. This is the kind of thing that your mother wanted to know when she asked, "What did you learn in school today?" If you understand the big picture, then all the details, terminology, and formulas will be much easier to learn. Keep in mind, however, that the summary does not include all of the individual topics that are covered in the chapter. You will need to read the complete chapter and work some of the problems before you will pick up all the details.

Learning Objectives. Next we provide a list of goals that should be achieved upon completion of studying a text chapter. These objectives usually are task-oriented, pointing to specific things you should know how to do or how to explain. If you lack confidence in meeting any of these objectives, you should return to the appropriate section(s) of the text for further study.

New Terms And Concepts. This section consists of a list of important terms and concepts that appeared in the text. You should identify or define these terms, and explain how closely-related terms are interrelated. Return to the text to check your answers.

<u>New Formulas</u>.   A list of formulas that were introduced in
the text is provided. For each formula, you should test
yourself in the following way:

   1) Identify each symbol and term in the formula.

   2) Make a list of the computational steps that are
   indicated by the formula.

   3) Describe when each formula is used and explain why
   it is used or what it is computing.

   4) Most importantly, you should realize that each
   formula is simply a concise, mathematical expression of
   a concept or procedure. If you can explain the concept
   or procedure <u>in words</u>, then it is usually very easy to
   translate the words into mathematical symbols and
   recreate the formula. Thus, we encourage you to
   understand concepts rather than memorize formulas.

<u>Step-By-Step</u>.   This section presents a typical problem (or
problems) from the chapter and provides a demonstration of
the step-by-step procedures for solving the problem.

<u>Hints and Cautions</u>.   In this section, we provide advice on
the typical mistakes students make, and the difficulties
they commonly have with the chapter material.

<u>Self-Test and Review</u>.   In this section we present a series
of questions and problems that provide a general review of
the chapter. As much as possible, the problems consist of
simple sets of numbers so that you can solve them with
minimal calculation. Work through this Self-Test carefully,
and remember that your mistakes will tell you what areas
need additional study. Incidentally, the <u>Answers</u> to the
Self-Test are given at the end of each Study Guide chapter.
For problems with numerical answers, do not fret about
slight differences between your answer and ours. A little
rounding error is to be expected.

STUDY HINTS

It seems appropriate for a study guide to have a few suggestions to help you study. The following are some hints that have proved useful for our own students.

1.   You will learn (and remember) much more if you study for short periods several times a week, rather than concentrating all your studying into one long session. For example, it is far more effective to study for one-half hour every night than to spend a single 3 and one-half hour session once a week.

2.   Do some work before class. Read the appropriate sections in the textbook before your instructor presents the material in class. Although you may not completely understand what you read, you will have a general idea of the topic which will make the lecture easier to follow. Also, you can identify items that are particularly confusing and then be sure that these items are clarified in class.

3.   Pay attention and think during class. Although this may sound like obvious advice, many students spend their class time frantically taking notes rather than listening and understanding what is being said. For example, it usually is not necessary to copy down every sample problem that your instructor works in class. There are plenty of example problems in your textbook and in this study guide - you probably do not need one more in your notebook. Just put down your pencil and pay attention. Be sure that you understand what is being done, and try to anticipate the next step in the problem.

4.   Test yourself regularly. Do not wait until the end of the chapter or the end of the week to check your knowledge. After each lecture, work some of the end-of-chapter problems, do the learning checks, and be sure you can define key terms. If you are having trouble, get your questions answered immediately (re-read the text, go to your instructor, ask questions in class). Do not let yourself fall behind.

5.   Don't kid yourself. Many students sit in class watching the instructor solve problems, and think to themselves, "This looks easy, I understand it." Do you really? Can you do the problem all by yourself?

Many students use the examples in the textbook as a guide for working assigned problems. They begin the problem, get stuck, then check the example to see what to do next. A minute later they are stuck again, so they take another peek at the example in the text. Eventually, the problem is finished and the students think that they understand how to solve problems. Although there is nothing wrong with using examples as models for solving problems, you should try working a problem with your book closed to determine whether you can complete it on your own.

Finally a few tips to help you prepare for exams.

1.   Perhaps the best way to get ready for an exam is to make up your own exam. This is particularly effective if you have a friend in the class so you can both make up exams and then exchange them. Constructing your own exam forces you to identify the important points in the material, and it makes you think about how exam questions might be phrased. It is very satisfying to open a statistics exam and find some questions that you wrote yourself the day before.

2.   Many students suffer from "exam anxiety" which causes them to freeze up and forget everything during exams. One way to help avoid the problem is for you to take charge of your own time during an exam.

   a. Don't spend a lot of time working on one problem that you really don't understand (especially if it is a 1-point true/false question). Just move on to the rest of the exam - you can come back later, if you have time.

   b. Remember that you do not have to finish the exam questions in the order they are presented. When you get your exam, go immediately to the problems you understand best. This will build some confidence and make you better prepared for the remainder of the exam.

Probably the best way to reduce exam anxiety is to practice taking exams. Make up your own exam (select problems from the book and study guide) or have a friend make up an exam. Then try to duplicate the general conditions of an exam. If you are not allowed to use your book during exams, then put it away during practice. Give yourself a time limit. If you have an old alarm clock, set it in front of you so that you can hear the ticking and watch the time slip away. You might even try sitting in front of a mirror so that every time you look up there is someone watching you.

Finally, remember that very few miracles happen during exams. The work on your exam is usually a good reflection of your studying and understanding. Most students walk into an exam with a very good idea of how well they will do. Be honest with yourself. If you are well prepared, you will do well on the exam, and there is no reason to panic. If you are not prepared then exam anxiety probably is not your problem.

CHAPTER 1

INTRODUCTION TO STATISTICS

CHAPTER SUMMARY

The general goals of Chapter 1 are:

1. To introduce the basic terminology that will be used in statistics.

2. To explain how statistical techniques fit into the general process of science.

3. To introduce some of the notation that will be used throughout the rest of the book.

TERMINOLOGY

A <u>variable</u> is a characteristic or condition that can change or take on different values. Most research begins with a general question about the relationship between two variables for a specific group of individuals. The entire group of individuals is called the <u>population</u>. For example, a researcher may be interested in the relation between class size (variable 1) and academic performance (variable 2) for the population of third-grade children. Usually populations are so large that a researcher cannot examine the entire group, Therefore, a <u>sample</u> is selected to represent the population in a research study.

Variables can be classified as discrete or continuous. Discrete variables (such as class size) consist of indivisible categories, and continuous variables (such as time or weight) are infinitely dividable into whatever units a researcher may choose. For example, time can be measured to the nearest minute, second, half-second, etc.) To define the units for a continuous variable, a researcher must use real limits which are boundaries located exactly half-way between adjacent categories.

To establish relationships between variables, researchers must observe the variables and record their observations. This requires that the variables be measured. The process of measuring a variable requires a set of categories called a scale of measurement and a process that classifies each individual into one category. Four types of measurement scales are as follows:

a. A nominal scale is an unordered set of categories identified only by name. Nominal measurements only permit you to determine whether two individuals are the same or different.

b. An ordinal scale is an ordered set of categories. Ordinal measurements tell you the direction of difference between two individuals.

c. An interval scale is an ordered series of equal-sized categories. Interval measurements identify the direction and magnitude of a difference.

d. A ratio scale is an interval scale where a value of zero indicates none of the variable. Ratio measurements identify the direction and magnitude of differences and allow ratio comparisons of measurements.

Research studies can be classified as experiments, correlational studies, or quasi-experimental studies. In an experiment, one variable is manipulated and a second variable is observed to determine whether the manipulation causes changes. All other variables are controlled to prevent them from influencing the results. In an experiment, the manipulated variable is called the <u>independent variable</u> and the observed variable is the <u>dependent variable</u>. A <u>correlational</u> study simply observes the two variables as they exist naturally. A <u>quasi-experimental</u> study is similar to an experiment but is missing either the manipulation or the control necessary for a true experiment. Quasi-experimental studies are classified as <u>differential</u> (comparing pre-existing groups) or <u>time-series</u> (comparing changes over time).

STATISTICS IN SCIENCE

The measurements obtained in a research study are called the <u>data</u>. The goal of statistics is to help researchers organize and interpret the data. Statistical techniques are classified into two broad categories: descriptive and inferential. <u>Descriptive statistics</u> are methods for organizing and summarizing data. For example, tables or graphs are used to organize data, and descriptive values such as the average score are used to summarize data. A descriptive value for a population is called a <u>parameter</u> and a descriptive value for a sample is called a <u>statistic</u>. <u>Inferential statistics</u> are methods for using sample data to make general conclusions (inferences) about populations. Because a sample is typically only a part of the whole population, sample data provide only limited information about the population. As a result, sample statistics are generally imperfect representatives of the corresponding population parameters. The discrepancy between a sample statistic and its population parameter is called <u>sampling error</u>. Defining and measuring sampling error is a large part of inferential statistics.

NOTATION

The individual measurements or scores obtained for a subject will be identified by the letter X (or X and Y if there are multiple scores per subject). The number of scores in a data set will be identified by <u>N</u> for a population or <u>n</u> for a sample.

Summing a set of values is a common operation in statistics and has its own notation. The Greek letter sigma, Σ, will be used to stand for "the sum of." For example, ΣX identifies the sum of the scores. To use and interpret summation notation, you must follow the basic <u>order of operations</u> required for all mathematical calculation.

1. All calculations within parentheses are done first.
2. Squaring, multiplying, and dividing are done second, and should be completed in order from left to right.
3. Adding and subtracting (including summation) are third, and should be completed in order from left to right.

For example, to compute $\Sigma X + 3$, you sum the X values, then add 3. To compute $\Sigma(X + 3)^2$, you add 3 to each X (inside parentheses), then square the resulting values, then sum the squared numbers.

LEARNING OBJECTIVES

---

1. You should be familiar with the terminology and special notation of statistical methods.

2. You should understand the purpose of statistics: When, how, and why they are used.

3. You should understand summation notation and be able to use this notation to represent mathematical operations and to compute specified sums.

NEW TERMS AND CONCEPTS

The following terms were introduced in Chapter 1. Define or describe each term and, where appropriate, describe how each term is related to other terms in the list.

population	control group
sample	experimental group
statistic	hypothetical construct
parameter	operational definition
sampling error	nominal scale
descriptive statistics	ordinal scale
inferential statistics	interval scale
variable	ratio scale
constant	discrete variable
raw score	continuous variable
dependent variable	Σ (sigma)
independent variable	N
correlational method	n
experimental method	X
quasi-experimental method	Y

STEP BY STEP

Summation Notation: In statistical calculations you constantly will be required to add a set of values to find a specific total. We will use algebraic expressions to represent the values being added (for example, X = score), and we will use the Greek letter sigma (Σ) to signify the process of summation. Occasionally, you simply will be adding a set of scores, ΣX. More often, you will be doing some initial computation and then adding the results. For example, we will routinely need to square each score and then find the sum of the squared values, ΣX^2. The following step-by-step process should help you understand summation notation and use it correctly to find appropriate totals.

Step 1: The first step in using summation correctly is to identify the "term" or "algebraic expression" that follows the summation sign. There are 3 general rules to help you identify the "term."

a. Everything contained within parentheses is part of the same term.

b. If several things are being multiplied together, they are all part of the same term.

c. If something is squared, the squared sign is part of the term.

Step 2:   Set up a computational table listing the original X values in the first column. Use the "term" you identified from Step 1 as a new column heading, and list all of the appropriate values for this term under the new heading.

Suppose your task is to find $\Sigma(X + 3)$. The "term" in this expression is $(X + 3)$, so use this as a column heading and list all of the $(X + 3)$ values next to the original X values.

X	(X + 3)
4	7
8	11
2	5
6	9

Note: Occasionally you will need more than one column to get to the final term you want. To compute $\Sigma(X + 3)^2$, for example, begin with the X column, then add a column of $(X + 3)$ values, and then add a third column that squares each of the (X + 3) values. Thus, each column represents a step in the computations.

X	(X + 3)	$(X + 3)^2$
4	7	49
8	11	121
2	5	25
6	9	81

Step 3: Simply add all the values in the column headed by the term identified in Step 1.

Using the same numbers that we used in Step 2, you find $\Sigma(X + 3)$ by simply adding the values in the (X + 3) column.

$$\Sigma(X + 3) = 7 + 11 + 5 + 9 = 32$$

To find $\Sigma(X + 3)^2$ you add the values in the $(X + 3)^2$ column.

$$\Sigma(X + 3)^2 = 49 + 121 + 25 + 81 = 276.$$

HINTS AND CAUTIONS

1. Many students confuse the independent variable and the dependent variable in an experiment. It may help you to differentiate these terms if you visualize an experiment as a big black box filled with people.
   Independent Variable: The scientist (in a white lab-coat) stands outside the box and independently manipulates things (visualize knobs on the box that control things like temperature, background noise, etc.). The variable manipulated by the scientist is the independent variable.

Dependent Variable: Meanwhile, the purpose of the experiment is to see whether the people inside the box will respond to the scientist's manipulations. In other words, will the people's responses depend on what the scientist is doing. The dependent variable is the set of responses that the scientist observes and measures.

2.   There are three specific sums that are used repeatedly in statistics calculations. You should know the notation and computations for each of the following:

   a. ΣX^2 First square each score, then add the squared values.
   b. $(\Sigma X)^2$ First sum the scores, then square the total.
   c. $\Sigma(X - C)^2$ First subtract the constant C from each score, then square each of the resulting values. Finally, add the squared numbers.

SELF-TEST AND REVIEW

---

1.   Statistical procedures that attempt to simplify and summarize data are classified as _____ statistics.

2.   Statistical procedures that use sample data as the basis for answering general questions about populations are called _____ statistics.

3.   A characteristic (usually a single number) that describes a sample is called a _____.

4.   One characteristic of an experiment is that the researcher manipulates one of the variables being examined. (True or False)

5.   A researcher wants to examine the relationship between family size and political attitude for a group of 100 college students. Each student is asked to report the number of individuals in his/her immediate family and each student completes an attitude questionnaire that measures political opinions. Does this study use the correlational method or the experimental method?

6.   A recent study reports that infant rats fed a special protein-enriched diet reached an adult weight 10% greater than litter-mates raised on a regular diet. For this study, what is the independent variable? What is the dependent variable?

7.   Classifying a sample into two groups, males and females, is an example of measurement on a nominal scale. (True or False)

8.   Classifying a sample of students according to high, medium, and low self-esteem would be an example of measurement on an interval scale. (True or False)

9.   To compute $\Sigma X - 1$, you first subtract one point from each score and then sum the resulting values. (True or False)

10.   Compute each value requested for the following set of scores.

X		
1	ΣX =	_____
3	ΣX^2 =	_____
5	$(\Sigma X)^2$ =	_____
2	N =	_____

11. Compute each value requested for the following set of scores.

	X			
	0	$\Sigma X + 1$	=	_____
	6	$\Sigma(X + 1)$	=	_____
	2	$\Sigma(X + 1)^2$	=	_____
	3			

12. Use summation notation to express each of the following calculations.

    a.   Add 3 points to each score, then find the sum of the resulting values.

    b.   Find the sum of the scores, then add 10 points to the total.

    c.   Subtract 1 point from each score, then square each of the resulting values. Next, find the sum of the squared numbers. Finally, add 5 points to this sum.

====================

ANSWERS TO SELF-TEST

====================

1.   Descriptive statistics

2.   Inferential statistics

3.   Statistic

4.   True

5.   This is a correlational study. The researcher is observing variables that exist naturally. There is no manipulation.

6. The independent variable is the diet (manipulated) and the
    dependent variable is the weight measured for each rat.

7. True

8. False. The measurements are on an ordinal scale.

9. False. The notation instructs you to sum the scores and
    then subtract 1 point from the total.

10. $\Sigma X = 11$, $\Sigma X^2 = 39$, $(\Sigma X)^2 = 121$, $N = 4$

11. $\Sigma X + 1 = 11 + 1 = 12$
    $\Sigma(X + 1) = 1 + 7 + 3 + 4 = 15$
    $\Sigma(X + 1)^2 = 1 + 49 + 9 + 16 = 75$

12. a. $\Sigma(X + 3)$
    b. $\Sigma X + 10$
    c. $\Sigma(X - 1)^2 + 5$

CHAPTER 2

FREQUENCY DISTRIBUTIONS

CHAPTER SUMMARY

After collecting data, the first task for a researcher is
to organize and simplify the data so that it is possible to get a
general overview of the results. This is the goal of descriptive
statistical techniques. One method for simplifying and
organizing data is to construct a frequency distribution. Chapter
2 presents the general concept of a frequency distribution and
explains several methods for constructing and displaying these
distributions. In any given set of scores, we can determine how
often a value is observed. "How often" is the frequency for that
value. For example, a set of N = 5 scores consist of 3, 2, 2,
1, 2. For these data, the value X = 2 is observed three times.
Therefore its frequency is f = 3. Frequency distributions are
commonly presented in tables and graphs.

Frequency Distribution Tables: Frequency distribution
tables contain at least two columns - one for X and another for f
(frequency). In the X column values are listed from the highest
to lowest, without skipping any. For the frequency column,
tallies are determined for each value (how often each X value
occurs in the data set. These tallies are the frequencies for
each X value. The sum of the frequencies should equal N. A

third column can be used for proportion (p). That is, we can determine what proportion of the entire data set consists a particular X value. For any X value, $p = f/N$. The sum of the p column should equal 1.00. Finally, a fourth column displays the percentage of the distribution that any X value represents. The percentage is found by multiplying p by 100. The sum of this column, of course, should be 100%.

Sometimes a data set has a very wide range of values. In these situations a list of the X values in the first column is quite long - too long to provide enough simplification of the data. To remedy this situation, grouped frequency distribution tables are used. In the X column, class intervals are listed from highest to lowest interval, without skipping any interval. These intervals all have the same width, determined by the difference between the upper and lower real limits. The interval begins with a value that is a multiple of the interval width. The interval width (such as 2, 5, 10, 20, 50, 100) is selected so that the table will have approximately ten intervals (7 to 15).

Frequency Distributions Graphs: Frequency distribution graphs take the information from a frequency distribution table and essentially gives us a "picture" of the data set. The horizontal axis (abscissa) represents values for X. The vertical axis (ordinate) is used for frequency and is labelled f. A histogram is a graph that uses bars. It is assumed that the X-axis is a continuous number line (reflecting measurement of a continuous variable). A bar is centered over each observed X value. The bar extends vertically to the corresponding frequency for that score. The width of the bar corresponds to the real limits of the X value. Thus, neighboring scores will have bars that touch.

A bar graph is like a histogram, except it is used with discrete variables. The bars for neighboring values or categories do not touch.

Polygons are graphs that may be used in place of histograms. Instead of using bars, a polygon places a dot centered above each X value. The vertical distance of the dot above X corresponds to the frequency for that score. The dots are then connected by straight lines and the lines are brought down to the X-axis at both ends of the graph.

Frequency distribution graphs are useful because they give us information about the shape of the distribution. A distribution is symmetrical if the left half of the graph is a mirror image of the right half. One example of a symmetrical distribution is the bell-shaped normal distribution. On the other hand, distributions are skewed when scores pile up on one side of the distribution, leaving a "tail" of a few extreme values on the other side. In a distribution with positive skew, the scores tend to pile up on the left side (low X values) of the distribution with the tail on the right. Negative skew is the opposite. Most of the scores have high values (right side of the distribution) and the tail points to the left.

Frequency distribution tables can be used to determine percentile rank. A percentile rank for a particular X value is the percentage of scores equal to and below that X value. The X value is called the percentile. To find a percentile rank, two new columns are placed in the frequency distribution table. One is for cumulative frequency (cf) and the other is for cumulative percent (c%). The cumulative percent of a score is its percentile rank.

LEARNING OBJECTIVES

1. Know how to organize data into regular or grouped frequency distribution tables.

2. Be able to construct graphs, including bar graphs, histograms, and polygons.

3.   Be able to describe the shape of a distribution
     portrayed in a frequency distribution graph.

NEW TERMS AND CONCEPTS

The following terms were introduced in this chapter.
Define or describe each term and, where appropriate, describe
how each term is related to other terms in the list.

    frequency distribution
    grouped frequency distribution
    class interval
    upper real limit
    lower real limit
    apparent limits
    histogram
    bar graph
    polygon
    symmetrical distribution
    positively skewed distribution
    negatively skewed distribution
    tail(s) of a distribution
    stem and leaf display
    percentile
    percentile rank
    cumulative frequency (cf)
    cumulative percent (c%)
    interpolation

NEW FORMULAS

    proportion = p = f/N
    percentage = p(100) = (f/N)(100)
    cumulative percent = (cf/N)(100)

Constructing a Frequency Distribution Table: The goal of a frequency distribution table is to take an entire set of scores and simplify and organize them into a form that allows a researcher to see at a glance the entire distribution. Suppose, for example, that an instructor gave a personality questionnaire measuring self-esteem to an entire class of psychology students. The questionnaire classifies each individual into one of five categories indicating different levels of self esteem: 1 = high self-esteem and 5 = low self-esteem. The results for the class are as follows:

           4, 4, 3, 3, 5, 4, 2, 1, 1, 3
           4, 4, 5, 2, 3, 3, 4, 3, 3, 2
           1, 4, 5, 3, 4, 4, 5, 2, 4, 1
           3, 3, 2, 2, 4, 5, 1, 5, 3, 4

Step 1: In the first column of the table, list the scale of measurement starting with the highest score at the top and listing every possible X value down to the lowest score. The column heading should be "X" to indicate that this is the scale of X values.

X
5
4
3
2
1

Step 2: In a second column, headed by "f" for frequency, list the number of individuals who have each score. For example, six people have scores of X = 5, so you place a 6 in the f column beside the X value 5. Continue for each score (category) on the scale of measurement.

X	f
5	6
4	12
3	11
2	6
1	5

The result is a basic frequency distribution table. The
table can be expanded by adding columns for proportion or
percentage.

Retrieving Scores from a Frequency Distribution Table:
Although a frequency distribution table provides a concise
overview of an entire set of data, it is a condensed version of
the actual data and for some students the table can obscure the
details of the individual scores. For example, in the table we
have just constructed, a set of 40 individual scores has been
condensed into a table that shows only 10 numerical values (five
X's and five frequencies). For some purposes, it   is easier
to transform a frequency distribution table back into a complete
set of scores before you begin any statistical calculations with
the data. We will use the table we have already constructed to
demonstrate the process of recovering individual scores from a
frequency distribution table.

Step 1: Find the number of individual scores (N): The
frequency column (f) of the table shows the number of
individuals located in each category on the scale of
measurement. For this example, six individuals had scores
of X = 5, twelve individuals had scores of X = 4, and so on.
To determine the total number of individuals in the group,
you simply add the frequencies.

$$N = \Sigma f = 6 + 12 + 11 + 6 + 5 = 40$$

Step 2: List the complete set of individual scores: Again, the table shows that six individual had scores of X = 5, twelve individuals had X = 4, and so on. These scores can be listed individually as follows:

5, 5, 5, 5, 5, 5	six fives
4, 4, 4, 4, 4, 4, 4, 4, 4, 4, 4, 4	twelve fours
3, 3, 3, 3, 3, 3, 3, 3, 3, 3, 3	eleven threes
2, 2, 2, 2, 2, 2	six twos
1, 1, 1, 1, 1	five ones

With the complete set of N = 40 scores listed in this way it is easy to perform computations based on individual scores. For example, to find ΣX you would add the 40 values ($\Sigma X = 128$).

Interpolation: Because it is impossible to report an infinite number of data points, nearly all tables and graphs show only a limited number of selected values. However, researchers often want to examine data points that fall between the reported values. The process of interpolation provides a method for estimating intermediate values.

In this chapter we used interpolation to find percentiles and percentile ranks that cannot be read directly from a frequency distribution table. The following example will be used to demonstrate this process.

The problem is to find the 50th percentile for the distribution shown in the following table. Because 50% is not one of the cumulative percentages listed in the table (it is between 20% and 65%), we must use interpolation.

X	f	cf	c%
25-29	1	20	100%
20-24	1	19	95%
15-19	5	18	90%
10-14	9	13	65%
5-9	4	4	20%

Step 1:   Identify the interval that contains the
intermediate value you want.   In this example we are looking
for the score that has a rank of 50%.   The intermediate
value, 50%, is located between the reported values of 20%
and 65%.

Step 2:   Draw a sketch showing the interval you identified
in Step 1.   Show the two end points of the interval and
identify the location of the intermediate value.

<u>c%</u>

65%

---50%

20%

Step 3:   Expand your sketch by placing the second scale
beside the one you have drawn.   Then find the end-points of
the interval on the second scale.   Remember, each cumulative
percentage value is associated with the upper real limit of
the score interval.

<u>X</u>	<u>c%</u>
14.5	65%

?----   ---50%

9.5   20%

Step 4:   Look at your sketch and make a common-sense
estimate of the final answer.   In this example, the value we
want is between 14.5 and 9.5.   It appears to be closer to
14.5, probably around X = 13.   (This kind of preliminary
estimate can save you from making a careless mistake later.)

Step 5:   Find the precise location of the intermediate value
within the interval.   This step requires that you compute a
fraction,

$$\text{fraction} = \frac{\text{distance from the top of the interval}}{\text{interval width}}$$

For this example, the intermediate value of 50% is located 15 points from the top of the interval and the interval width is 45 points (from 65% to 20%).   Thus,

$$\text{fraction} = 15/45 = 1/3 = 0.33$$

The position we want is located 1/3rd of the way down from the top of the interval.

Step 6:   Apply the fraction from Step 5 to the other scale. In this case we want to find the point that is 1/3rd of the way down from the top on the score side of the interval. The total distance on the score side is 5 points, so the position we want is

$$(1/3)(5) = 1.67 \text{ points down from the top}$$

Step 7:   Compute the final value by starting at the top of the interval and subtracting the distance you computed in Step 6.   In this example, the top of the score interval is 14.5 and we want to come down 1.67 points.   The final answer is,

$$14.50 - 1.67 = 12.83$$

We have determined that a percentile rank of 50% corresponds to a score of 12.83.   Notice that this answer is in agreement with the preliminary estimate of X = 13 that we made in Step 4.   (If there is a contradiction between your answer and your estimate, you should check your calculations.)

HINTS AND CAUTIONS

1. When making the list of intervals for a grouped frequency distribution table, some people find it easier to begin the list with the lowest interval and work up to the highest. Fewer mistakes will be made.

2. When interpreting a frequency distribution table, be sure to use both columns, X and f, to get a complete list of the entire set of scores. Remember, the X column does not list all the scores, it simply shows the scale of measurement.

SELF-TEST AND REVIEW

1. Simplifying and organizing data is the goal of descriptive statistics. One descriptive technique is to organize a set of scores in a frequency distribution. Define a frequency distribution and explain how it simplifies and organizes data.

2. Occasionally it is necessary to group scores into class intervals and construct a grouped frequency distribution.
   a. Explain when it is necessary to use a grouped table (as opposed to a regular table).
   b. Outline the guidelines for constructing a grouped frequency table.

3. A frequency distribution graph can be either a histogram, a bar graph, or a polygon. Define each of these graphs and identify the circumstances where each is used.

4.   For a continuous variable each score actually corresponds to an interval on the scale of measurement.

   a.   In general terms define the real limits of an interval.

   b.   If a distribution has scores of 10, 9, 8, etc., what are the real limits for X = 8?

   c.   If a distribution has scores of 5.5, 5.0, 4.5, 4.0, etc., what are the real limits for X = 4.5?

   d.   In a grouped frequency distribution, each class interval has real limits and apparent limits. What are the real and apparent limits for the interval 10-14?

5.   For the following set of scores:

        8, 7, 10, 12, 9, 11, 10, 9, 12, 11

        7, 9, 7, 10, 10, 8, 12, 7, 10, 7

   a.   Construct a frequency distribution table including columns for frequency, proportion, and percentage.

   b.   Draw a histogram showing these data.

   c.   Draw a polygon showing the data.

6.   A set of data have a high score of X = 64 and a low score of X = 43. What interval width should be used for a grouped frequency distribution table? List all of the intervals.

7.   Construct a stem-and-leaf display for the following data. What is the shape of the distribution?

        83   46   32   44   75   35   33   47   54   72   60   22

        48   57   49   67   25   51   92   84   43   50   36   40

Questions 8 - 11 are for the following data:

X	f
5	1
4	2
3	2
2	4
1	3

8. The sum of X is 15. (True or False)

9. N equals _____
    a. 5
    b. 12
    c. not enough information is given

10. The cumulative frequency (cf) for X = 4 is
    a. 2   b. 6   c. 11

11. The percentile rank for X = 3.5 is
    a. 58%   b. 50%   c. 75%   d. 90%

12. Consider the data in the following table.

X	f	cf	c%
55-59	1	25	100
50-54	2	24	96
45-49	2	22	88
40-44	2	20	80
35-39	4	18	72
30-34	5	14	56
25-29	2	9	36
20-24	4	7	28
15-19	2	3	12
10-14	1	1	4

a. Find the 50th percentile for this distribution.

b. Find the 60th percentile.

c. What is the percentile rank for X = 42?

d. What is the percentile rank for 44.5?

13. Census data show that most people earn small to moderate wages while a few people have most of the wealth. The frequency distribution for income is

     a. negatively skewed

     b. positively skewed

     c. symmetrical

=====================

ANSWERS TO SELF-TEST

=====================

1. A frequency distribution shows the number of individuals located in each category on the scale of measurement.

2. a. A grouped frequency distribution table is needed when the range of scores is large, causing a frequency distribution table to have to many entries in the X column.

   b. In a grouped frequency distribution table the guidelines are

      1. You should strive for approximately 10 rows in the table (7 - 15).

      2. Interval widths of 2, 5, 10, 20, 50, and 100 should be used. (Select the interval width that satisfies guideline 1.) Interval width is determined by the difference between the real limits of the class interval.

      3. The first (lowest) value of each interval should be a multiple of the interval width.

4. List all intervals without skipping any. The top interval should contain the highest observed X value and the bottom interval should contain the lowest observed X value.

3. In a histogram there is a bar above each score (or interval) showing the frequency. Adjacent bars are touching. A histogram is used with interval or ratio data. A bar graph is similar to a histogram except that there are spaces between the bars and the bar graph is used with nominal or ordinal data. In a polygon, the frequency is indicated by a dot above each score (or interval), and the dots are connected with straight lines. A polygon is used with interval or ratio data.

4. a. The real limits for a score are the boundaries located halfway between the score and the next higher (or lower) score.
   b. The real limits for X = 8 would be 7.5 and 8.5.
   c. For X = 4.5, the real limits would be 4.25 and 4.75.
   d. For the class interval 10-14, the real limits are 9.5 and 14.5. The apparent limits are 10 and 14.

5. a.

X	f	p	%
12	3	.15	15%
11	2	.10	10%
10	5	.25	25%
9	3	.15	15%
8	2	.10	10%
7	5	.25	25%

b.

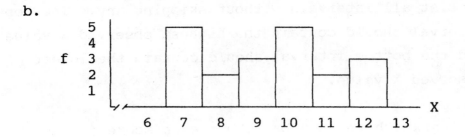

c.

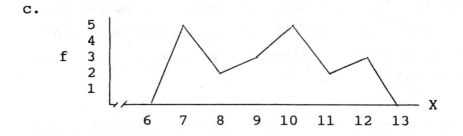

6.   An interval width of 2 results in 12 intervals. An interval width of 5 results in only 5 intervals.

X	X
64-65	60-64
62-63	55-59
60-61	50-54
58-59	45-49
56-57	40-44
54-55	
52-53	
50-51	
48-49	
46-47	
44-45	
42-43	

7.

2	25
3	2536
4	6478930
5	4710
6	07
7	52
8	34
9	2

The distribution is positively skewed.

8. False. You must use <u>both</u> the X and f columns to determine the sum of X for the distribution. $\Sigma X = 30$.

9. $\Sigma f = N = 12$

10. $cf = 11$

11. $c\% = 75\%$

12. a. $X = 33$
    b. $X = 35.75$
    c. $c\% = 76\%$
    d. $c\% = 80\%$

13. It is positively skewed because most scores (incomes) pile up on the left side of the distribution with the tail of extreme values pointing to the right side (positive direction on the number line).

CHAPTER 3

CENTRAL TENDENCY

The purpose of Chapter 3 is to introduce the concept of central tendency and the three different statistical procedures that are used to define and measure central tendency. In general terms, central tendency is a statistical measure that determines a single value that accurately describes and represents an entire distribution of scores. The goal of central tendency is to identify the single value that is the best representative for the entire set of data.

By identifying the "average score," central tendency allows researchers to summarize or condense a large set of data into a single value. Thus, central tendency serves as a descriptive statistic because it allows researchers to describe or present a set of data in a very simplified, concise form. For example, the reading ability for an entire third-grade class can be summarized by the average reading score. In addition, it is possible to compare two (or more) sets of data by simply comparing the average score (central tendency) for one set versus the average score for another set. For example, a report may summarize research results by stating that the patients who received medication had an average cholesterol level 50 points lower than patients without medication.

It is essential that central tendency be determined by an objective and well-defined procedure so that others will understand exactly how the "average" value was obtained and can duplicate the process. Because no single procedure always produces a good, representative value, there are three commonly used techniques for measuring central tendency: the mean, the median, and the mode.

The Mean: The mean is the most commonly used measure of central tendency. Computation of the mean requires scores that are numerical values, usually measured on an interval or ratio scale. The mean is obtained by computing the sum, or total, for the entire set of scores, then dividing this sum by the number of scores.

For sample data the mean is: $\bar{X} = \dfrac{\Sigma X}{n}$

For population data the mean is: $\mu = \dfrac{\Sigma X}{N}$

Conceptually, the mean can also be defined as:
1. The mean is the amount that each individual receives when the total (ΣX) is divided equally among all N individuals.
2. The mean is the balance point of the distribution because the sum of the distances below the mean is exactly equal to the sum of the distances above the mean.

Because the calculation of the mean involves every score in the distribution, changing the value of any score will change the value of the mean. Also, modifying a distribution by discarding scores or by adding new scores will usually change the value of the mean. To determine how the mean will be affected for any specific situation you must consider: 1) how the number of scores is affected, and 2) how the sum of the scores is affected. For example, adding a new score to a distribution will increase the number of scores by 1, and will increase ΣX by the value of the new score.

If a constant value is added to every score in a distribution, then the same constant value is added to the mean. Also, if every score is multiplied by a constant value, then the mean is also multiplied by the same constant value.

Although the mean is the most commonly used measure of central tendency, there are situations where the mean does not provide a good, representative value, and there are situations where you cannot compute a mean at all. When a distribution contains a few extreme scores (or is very skewed), the mean will be pulled toward the extremes (displaced toward the tail). In this case, the mean will not provide a "central" value. With data from a nominal scale it is impossible to compute a mean, and when data are measured on an ordinal scale (ranks), it is usually inappropriate to compute a mean. Thus, the mean does not always work as a measure of central tendency and it is necessary to have alternative procedures available.

The Median: The median is defined as the score or position in a distribution that divides the set of scores into two equal groups: exactly 50% of the scores are greater than the median, and exactly 50% are less than the median. Thus, the median is equal to the 50th percentile. Computation of the median requires scores that can be placed in rank order (smallest to largest) and are measured on an ordinal, interval, or ratio scale. Usually, the median can be found by a simple counting procedure:

1. With an even number of scores, list the values in order, and the median is the middle score in the list.

2. With an even number of scores, list the values in order, and the median is half-way between the middle two scores.

Often the simplest method for finding the median is to place the scores in a frequency distribution histogram with each score represented by a box in the graph. The goal is to draw a vertical line through the distribution so that exactly half the boxes are on each side of the line. The median is defined by the location of the line.

One advantage of the median is that it is relatively unaffected by extreme scores. Thus, the median tends to stay in the "center" of the distribution even when there are a few extreme scores or when the distribution is very skewed. In these situation, the median serves as a good alternative to the mean.

The Mode: The mode is defined as the most frequently occurring category or score in the distribution. In a frequency distribution graph, the mode is the category or score corresponding to the peak or high point of the distribution. The mode can be determined for data measured on any scale of measurement: nominal, ordinal, interval, or ratio.

It is possible for a distribution to have more than one mode. For example, a frequency distribution graph may have two peaks, with a mode at each peak. Such a distribution is called bimodal. (Note that a

distribution can have only one mean and only one median.)
In addition, the term "mode" is often used to describe a
peak in a distribution that is not really the highest
point. Thus, a distribution may have a major mode at the
highest peak and a minor mode at a secondary peak in a
different location.

The primary value of the mode is that it is the only
measure of central tendency that can be used for data
measured on a nominal scale. In addition, the mode often
is used as a supplemental measure of central tendency
that is reported along with the mean or the median.

Because the mean, the median, and the mode are all measuring
central tendency, the three measures are often systematically
related to each other. In a symmetrical distribution, for
example, the mean and median will always be equal. If a
symmetrical distribution has only one mode, the mode, mean, and
median will all have the same value. In a skewed distribution,
the mode will be located at the peak on one side and the mean
will be displaced toward the tail on the other side. The median
will be located between the mean and the mode.

====================
LEARNING OBJECTIVES
====================

1.   You should be able to define central tendency and
     you should understand the general purpose of obtaining a
     measure of central tendency.

2.   You should be able to define and compute each of the three
     basic measures of central tendency for a set of data.

3. You should know how the mean is affected when a set of
    scores is modified. For example, what happens to the mean
    when a new score is added to an existing set, or when a
    score is removed, or when the value of a score is changed.
    In addition, you should know what happens to the mean when a
    constant value is added to every score in a distribution, or
    when every score is multiplied by a constant value.

4. You should know when each of the three measures of central
    tendency is used and you should understand the advantages
    and disadvantages of each.

5. You should know how the three measures of central tendency
    are related to each other for symmetrical distributions and
    for skewed distributions.

6. You should be able to draw and understand graphs showing the
    relationship between an independent variable and a dependent
    variable, where a measure of central tendency (usually the
    mean) is used to present the "average" score for the
    dependent variable.

NEW TERMS AND CONCEPTS

The following terms were introduced in this chapter.
Define or describe each term and, where appropriate, describe how
each term is related to other terms in the list.

central tendency
mean
median
mode (major mode and minor mode)
weighted mean

$$\mu = \frac{\Sigma X}{N}$$

$$\bar{X} = \frac{\Sigma X}{n}$$

====
STEP BY STEP
====

The Weighted Mean: Occasionally a researcher will find it necessary to combine two (or more) sets of data, or to add new scores to an existing set of data. Rather than starting from scratch to compute the mean for the new set of data, it is possible to compute the weighted mean. To find the new mean you need two pieces of information:

    1)   How many scores are in the new data set?

    2)   What is the sum of all the scores?

Remember, the mean is the sum of the scores divided by the number. We will use the following problem to demonstrate the calculation of the weighted mean.

A researcher wants to combine the following three samples into a single group. Notice that sample 3 is actually a single score, $X = 4$. What is the mean for the combined group?

Sample 1	Sample 2	Sample 3
$n = 8$	$n = 5$	$n = 1$
$\bar{X} = 12$	$\bar{X} = 9$	$\bar{X} = 4$

Step 1:   To find n and ΣX for the combined group, the first step is to find n and ΣX for each of the individual samples.

For example, sample 1 consists of n = 8 scores with a mean of $\bar{X}$ = 12. You can find ΣX for the scores by using the formula for the mean, and substituting the two values that you know,

$$\bar{X} = \frac{\Sigma X}{n}$$

In this case,

$$12 = \frac{\Sigma X}{8}$$

Multiplying both sides of the equation by 8 gives,

$$8(12) = \Sigma X$$
$$96 = \Sigma X$$

Often this process is easier to understand if you put dollar-signs on the numbers and remember that the mean is the amount that each individual receives if the total is divided equally. For this example, we have a group of 8 people (n) who have $12 each ($\bar{X}$). If the group puts all their money together (ΣX), how much will they have?   Again the answer is   ΣX = $96.

Step 2:   Repeat the process in Step 1 for each individual data set. If the problem involves adding a single score to an existing data set, then you can treat the single score as a sample with n = 1 and X = $\bar{X}$ = ΣX.

For this example, Sample 2 has a n = 5 and ΣX = 45, and Sample 3 has n = 1 and ΣX = 4.

Step 3:   Once you have determined n and ΣX for each
individual data set, then you simply add the individual
n's to find the number of scores in the combined set. In
the same way, you simply add the ΣX's to find the overall
sum of the scores in the combined data set. For this
example,

     combined n = 8 + 5 + 1 = 14
     combined ΣX = 96 + 45 + 4 = 145

Step 4:   Finally you compute the mean for the combined
group using the regular formula for $\bar{X}$.

$$\bar{X} = \Sigma X/n = 145/14 = 10.36$$

HINTS AND CAUTIONS

---

1.   One of the most common errors in computing central
tendency occurs when students are attempting to find the
mean for data in a frequency distribution table. You must
remember that the frequency distribution table condenses a
large set of scores into a concise, organized distribution;
the table does not list each of the individual scores. One
way of avoiding confusion is to transform the frequency
distribution table back into the original list of scores.
For example, the following frequency distribution table
presents a distribution for which three individuals had
scores of $X = 5$; one individual had $X = 4$; four individuals
had $X = 3$; no one had $X = 2$; and two individuals had $X = 1$.
When each of these scores is listed individually, it is much
easier to see that $N = 10$ and $\Sigma X = 33$ for these data.

Frequency Distribution		Original X Values
X	f	5
5	3	5
4	1	5
3	4	4
2	0	3
1	2	3
		3
		3
		1
		1

2.   Many students incorrectly assume that the median corresponds to the midpoint of the range of scores. For example, it is tempting to say that the median for a 100-point test would be X = 50. Be careful! The correct interpretation is that the median divides the set of scores (or individuals) into two equal groups. On a 100-point test, for example, the median could be X = 95 if the test was very easy and 50% of the class scored above 95. You must know where the individual scores are located before you can find the median.

Often is easy to locate the median if you sketch a histogram of the frequency distribution. If each score is represented by a "block" in the graph, you can find the median by positioning a vertical line so that it divides the blocks into two equal piles.

SELF-TEST AND REVIEW

1. Explain the general purpose for obtaining a measure of central tendency.

2. Explain why three different measures of central tendency are necessary - why isn't one standard procedure sufficient?

3. The primary measure of central tendency is the mean.
    a. In words, explain how the mean is computed.
    b. Identify the symbol and formula used for a population mean and for a sample mean.

4. Find N, ΣX, and μ for the set of scores in the following frequency distribution table.

X	f
5	2
4	1
3	4
2	3
1	2

5. If 10 points are added to each score in a population with $\mu = 80$, the new population will have a mean of _____.

6. For a population with $\mu = 30$, if each score is multiplied by 4, the resulting population will have a mean of _____.

7. If a sample of n = 8 scores has a mean of $\overline{X} = 6$, the total for this group must be $\Sigma X = $ ____.

8. A sample has $\Sigma X = 100$ and a mean of $\overline{X} = 20$. How many individuals are in the sample?

9. A distribution can have more than one _____ (mean, median, mode).

10. Changing the value of a single score in a distribution will always change the value of the _____ (mean, median, mode).

11. A sample of $n = 6$ scores has a mean of $\overline{X} = 10$.
   a. If a new score, $X = 3$, is added to the sample, what value will be obtained for the new sample mean?
   b. If one of the scores, $X = 20$, is removed from the original sample, what value would be obtained for the new sample mean?
   c. If one of the scores in the original sample is changed from $X = 6$ to $X = 24$, what value would be obtained for the new sample mean?

12. One sample has $n = 5$ and $\overline{X} = 20$. A second sample has $n = 15$ scores with $\overline{X} = 10$. If the two samples are combined, what is the value of the mean for the combined sample?

13. A distribution of scores has a mean of 84 and a median of 80. Based on this information it appears that the distribution is positively skewed. (True or False)

14. Compute the mean, median, and mode for the following set of scores.

   Scores: 5, 7, 5, 4, 3, 12, 9, 6, 6, 5, 7, 5, 6, 4

15. Compute the mean, median, and mode for the set of
    scores shown in the following frequency distribution
    table.

X	f
7	1
6	1
5	1
4	1
3	4
2	3
1	1

16. A researcher obtains the following results from an
experiment comparing three treatment conditions:

    Treatment #1: $\bar{X} = 12.7$

    Treatment #2: $\bar{X} = 20.5$

    Treatment #3: $\bar{X} = 8.4$

    a. Assuming that the independent variable (the differences
       between treatments) is measured on a nominal scale,
       sketch a graph showing the experimental results.
    b. Assuming that the independent variable is measured on
       an interval scale, sketch a graph showing the results.

ANSWERS TO SELF-TEST

1. The purpose of central tendency is to find a single
   value that best represents an entire distribution of
   scores.

2. No single procedure for measuring central tendency
   always provides a good representative value. For example, the mean can be displaced by extreme scores in a

distribution so that it is not a representative score. Also, there are situations where the mean cannot be calculated (for example, with open-ended distributions, undetermined scores, or data measured on a nominal scale). Thus, there are three different measures of central tendency that are intended to be used in different situations. Usually, at least one of these measures will provide a good representative value for the distribution.

3.   a. The mean is obtained by adding the scores to find the total, then dividing the total by the number of scores.
   b. The population mean is identified by μ, the Greek letter mu. The sample mean for a set of X values is identified by the symbol $\bar{X}$ ("X bar").

4.   N = Σf = 12. The 12 scores add to ΣX = 34, and the mean is μ = 34/12 = 2.83.

5. The new mean is 90. (10 points higher than the original mean.)

6. The new mean is 120. (The original mean is multiplied by 4.)

7. The total (ΣX) is 48. (If n = 8 individuals each have 6 points, then the total for the group must be 8 x 6 = 48.)

8. n = 5

9. It is possible for a distribution to have more than one mode. There can be only one mean and only one median for any distribution.

10. Changing a score will change the sum of the scores (ΣX) and, therefore, will change the mean.

11. a. With n = 6 and $\bar{X}$ = 10, the original sample has a total
         of ΣX = 60. Adding X = 3 produces n = 7 and ΣX = 63.
         The new mean is 63/7 = 9.

    b. With n = 6 and $\bar{X}$ = 10, the original sample has a total
        of ΣX = 60. Taking away X = 20 leaves a sample with n
        = 5 scores and ΣX = 40. The new mean is 40/5 = 8.

    c. Changing X = 6 to X = 24 adds 18 points to the total
        but does not change the number of scores. The new
        sample has n = 6 with ΣX = 78. The new mean is 78/6 =
        13.

12. The first sample has n = 5, $\bar{X}$ = 20, and ΣX = 100. The
second sample has n = 15, $\bar{X}$ = 10, and ΣX = 150. When the samples
are combined, the total number of score is n = 20 and the sum of
the scores is ΣX = 250. The mean for the combined sample is
250/20 = 12.5.

13. True. The mean is the higher value and is displaced toward
the tail. In this case, the tail is toward the higher end of the
distribution.

14. The mean is 84/14 = 6.00. The median is X = 5.5,
     and the mode is X = 5.

15. The mean is 41/12 = 3.42. The median is X = 3.00,
     and the Mode is X = 3.

16. a.

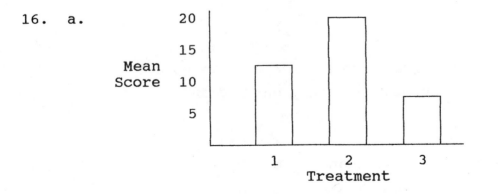

b. Use a histogram or a line graph (shown below).

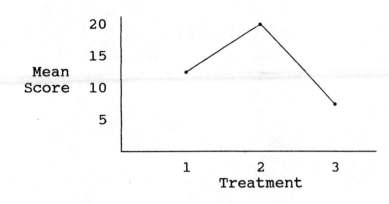

CHAPTER 4

VARIABILITY

This chapter introduces the statistical concept of variability and the different statistical methods for measuring it. The goal for variability is to obtain a measure of how spread out the scores are in a distribution. A measure of variability usually accompanies a measure of central tendency as basic descriptive statistics for a set of scores. Central tendency describes the central point of the distribution, and variability describes how the scores are scattered around that central point. Together, central tendency and variability are the two primary values that are used to describe a distribution of scores.

Variability serves both as a descriptive measure and as an important component of most inferential statistics. As a descriptive statistic, variability measures the degree to which the scores are spread out or clustered together in a distribution. In the context of inferential statistics, variability provides a measure of how accurately any individual score or sample represents the entire population. When the population variability is small, all of the scores are clustered close together and any individual score or sample will necessarily provide a good representation of the entire set. On the other hand, when variability is large and scores are widely spread, it is easy for one or two extreme scores to give a distorted picture of the general population.

Variability can be measured with the range, the interquartile range, or the standard deviation/variance. In each case, variability is determined by measuring distance. The range is the total distance covered by the distribution, from the highest score to the lowest score (using the upper and lower real limits of the range). The interquartile range is the distance covered by the middle 50% of the distribution (the difference between Q1 and Q3). Standard deviation measures the standard distance between a score and the mean. The calculation of standard deviation can be summarized as a four-step process:

a. Compute the deviation (distance from the mean) for each score.

b. Square each deviation.

c. Compute the mean of the squared deviations. For a population, this involves summing the squared deviations (sum of squares, SS) and then dividing by N. The answer value is called the variance or mean square and measures the average squared distance from the mean.

d. For samples, variance is computed by dividing the sum of the squared deviations (SS) by n - 1, rather than N. The value, n - 1, is know as degrees of freedom (df) and is used so that the sample variance will provide an unbiased estimate of the population variance.

e. Finally, take the square root of the variance to obtain the standard deviation.

1. Understand the measures of variability and be able to tell the difference between sets of scores with low versus high variability.

2. Know how to calculate SS using either the computational or definitional formula.

3. Be able to calculate the population and sample variance and standard deviation, and understand the correction used in the formulas for the sample statistics.

4. Be familiar with the characteristics of measures of variability, especially those for standard deviation.

===
NEW TERMS AND CONCEPTS
===

The following terms were introduced in this chapter. Define or describe each term and, where appropriate, describe how each term is related to other terms in the list.

> variability
> range
> first quartile
> third quartile
> semi-interquartile range
> deviation score
> population variance
> population standard deviation
> sample variance
> sample standard deviation
> unbiased estimate
> degrees of freedom

NEW FORMULAS

For a population:

$$SS = \Sigma(X - \mu)^2 \qquad \text{or} \qquad SS = \Sigma X^2 - \frac{(\Sigma X)^2}{N}$$

$$\sigma^2 = \frac{SS}{N} \qquad\qquad \sigma = \sqrt{\frac{SS}{N}}$$

For a sample:

$$SS = \Sigma(X - \bar{X})^2 \qquad \text{or} \qquad SS = \Sigma X^2 - \frac{(\Sigma X)^2}{n}$$

$$s^2 = \frac{SS}{n-1} \qquad\qquad s = \sqrt{\frac{SS}{n-1}} \qquad\qquad df = n - 1$$

STEP BY STEP

SS, Variance, and Standard Deviation: The following set of data will be used to demonstrate the calculation of SS, variance, and standard deviation.

Scores: 5, 3, 2, 4, 1

Step 1: Before you begin any calculation, simply look at the set of scores and make a preliminary estimate of the mean and standard deviation. For this set of data, it should be obvious that the mean is around 3, and most of the scores are within one or two points of the mean. Therefore, the standard deviation (standard distance from the mean) should be about 1 or 2.

Step 2:   Determine which formula you will use to compute SS.   If you have a relatively small set of data and the mean is a whole number, then use the definitional formula. Otherwise, the computational formula is a better choice. For this example there are only 5 scores and the mean is equal to 3.   The definitional formula would be fine for these scores.

Step 3:   Calculate SS.   Note that it does not matter whether the set of scores is a sample or a population when you are computing SS.   For this example, we will use formulas with population notation, but using sample notation would not change the result.

Definitional Formula: List each score in a column. In a second column put the deviation score for each X value. (Check that the deviations add to zero).   In a third column list the squared deviation scores.   Then simply add the values in the third column.

X	$(X - \mu)$	$(X - \mu)^2$
5	2	4
3	0	0
2	−1	1
4	1	1
1	−2	4
	0	10 = SS

Computational Formula: List each score in a column. In second column list the squared value for each X. Then find the sum for each column.   These are the two sums that are needed for the computational formula.

X	X²
5	25
3	9
2	4
4	16
1	1
15	55

$\Sigma X = 15$

$\Sigma X^2 = 55$

Then use the two sums in the computational formula to calculate SS.

$$SS = \Sigma X^2 - \frac{(\Sigma X)^2}{N}$$

$$= 55 - (15)^2/5 = 55 - 45$$

$$= 10$$

Step 4:   Now you must determine whether the set of scores is a sample or a population. With a population you use N in the formulas for variance and standard deviation. With a sample, use n - 1.

For a Population	For a Sample
$\sigma^2 = SS/N$	$s^2 = SS/(n-1)$
$= 10/5 = 2$	$= 10/4 = 2.5$
$\sigma = \sqrt{2} = 1.41$	$s = \sqrt{2.5} = 1.58$

HINTS AND CAUTIONS

1.   Mistakes are commonly made in the computational formula for SS. Often, ΣX^2 is confused with $(\Sigma X)^2$. The ΣX^2 indicates that the X values are first squared, then summed. On the other hand, $(\Sigma X)^2$ requires that the X values are first added, then the sum is squared.

2. Remember, it is impossible to get a negative value for SS because, by definition, SS is the sum of the squared deviation scores. The squaring operation eliminates all of the negative signs.

3. The computational formula is usually easier to use than the definitional formula because the mean usually is not a whole number.

4. When computing a variance or a standard deviation, be sure to check whether you are computing the measure for a population or a sample. Remember, the sample variance and standard deviation use $n - 1$ in the denominator so that these values will provide unbiased estimates of the corresponding population parameters.

5. Note that you do not use $n - 1$ in the formula for sample SS. The value $n - 1$ is used to compute sample variance and standard deviation after you have calculated SS.

====================

SELF-TEST AND REVIEW

====================

1. In this chapter we identified four measures of variability: the range, the semi-interquartile range, variance, and standard deviation.
   a. Define the basic purpose of a measure of variability.
   b. In words, define each of the four measures.

2. Explain how variance and standard deviation are related to the mean.

3. If a deviation score has a negative (-) sign, then the X value must be below the mean (True or False)

4. Deviation scores with high numerical values indicate that scores are clustered close to the mean. (True or False)

5. In a distribution with $\mu = 80$, which X value is further from the mean. One with a deviation score of -5, or one with a deviation score of +3.

6. For any distribution of scores, what value is always obtained for the sum of the deviation scores?
   a. sum = 0   b. sum > 0
   c. sum > or < 0   d. insufficient information

7. To compute either variance or standard deviation, you first must find the sum of the squared deviation scores - also called the sums of squares or simply SS.
   For the following set of scores, 5, 2, 8, 3
   a. Compute SS with the computational formula.
   b. Compute SS with the definitional formula.
   c. Which formula is better suited for these data? Explain your answer.
   d. Does the value you obtain for SS depend on whether these scores are a sample or a population?

8. Calculate the variance and standard deviation for the following sample of scores: 3, 3, 6, 8, 2, 6, 7, 5.

9. Compute the variance and standard deviation for the following population of scores: 8, 9, 5, 2, 6.

10. Sample variance is biased because it overestimates the population variance. (True or False)

11. Degrees of freedom (df) are used in the denominator of the formula for sample variance to obtain an unbiased estimate of population variance. (True or False)

12. The term "degrees of freedom" refers to the fact that all but one score in the population is free to vary. (True or False)

13. Calculate SS, variance, and standard deviation for the following sample of scores, 15, 16, 9, 1, 9.

14. Describe what happens to the deviation scores and the standard deviation when a constant is added to every score in the distribution.

═══════════
ANSWERS TO SELF-TEST
═══════════

1. a. The purpose of a measure of variability is to describe how spread out the scores are in a distribution.
     b. The range measures the distance from the largest to the smallest score. The semi-interquartile range measures one-half the distance from the first quartile to the third quartile. (That is, one-half the range covered by the middle 50% of the distribution.) Variance is the mean squared deviation. Standard deviation is the square root of the variance and measures the standard distance between a score and the mean.

2. Variance and standard deviation are based on deviation scores which measure the distance between each score and the mean.

3. True

4. False

5. -5   (5 points below the mean)

6. Answer a is correct. The sum of the deviation scores always equals zero. (Remember, the mean is the balance point of the distribution.)

7. a. With the computational formula $\Sigma X = 18$ and $\Sigma X^2 = 102$. SS = 21.

   b. The mean for the scores is 4.5, and the deviation scores are 0.5, -2.5, 3.5, and -1.5. The sum of squared deviations is SS = 21.

   c. The computational formula is better because the mean is not a whole number.

   d. No. The value obtained for SS is not influenced by whether the data are a sample or a population.

8. SS = 32, n = 8, df = 7, $s^2 = 4.57$, and s = 2.14.

9. SS = 30, n = 5, $\sigma^2 = 6$, $\sigma = 2.45$

10. False. The sample variance typically underestimates the population variance.

11. True

12. False. The concept of degrees of freedom, is based on the sample mean imposing a restriction on the variability of one score in the sample. Thus, n - 1 scores are free to vary.

13. SS = 144, $s^2 = 36$, and s = 6

14. If a constant is added to each score, the mean also in increased by that constant. The deviation scores are not changed. If the deviation scores have not changed, then the squared deviations and SS will be unchanged. Thus, when a constant is added to every score in a distribution, the standard deviation is not changed.

CHAPTER 5

z-SCORES

CHAPTER SUMMARY

Chapter 5 introduces the procedure for transforming scores (X values) into standardized z-scores. The process of changing X values into z-scores serves two purposes:

1. The z-score value specifies an exact location within a distribution.

2. Transforming X's to z-scores <u>standardizes</u> a distribution so that different distributions can be made comparable.

z-SCORES AND LOCATION

By itself, a raw score or X value provides very little information about how that particular score compares with other values in the distribution. A score of X = 53, for example, may be a relative low score, or an average score, or an extremely high score depending on the mean and standard deviation for the distribution from which the score was obtained. If the raw score is transformed into a z-score, however, the value of the z-score tells exactly where the score is located relative to all the other scores in the distribution. The process of changing an X value into a z-score involves creating a signed number, called a z-score, such that

    a. The sign of the z-score (+ or -) identifies whether the X value is located is above the mean (positive) or below the mean (negative).

    b. The numerical value of the z-score corresponds to the number of standard deviations between X and the mean of the distribution.

Thus, a score that is located two standard deviations above the mean will have a z-score of +2.00. And, a z-score of +2.00 always indicates a location above the mean by two standard deviations.

This basic definition is usually sufficient to complete most z-score transformations. However, the definition can be written in mathematical notation to create a formula for computing z-scores.

$$z = \frac{X - \mu}{\sigma}$$

Also, the terms in the formula can be regrouped to create an equation for computing the value of X corresponding to any specific z-score.

$$X = \mu + z\sigma$$

In addition to knowing the basic definition of a z-score and the formula for a z-score, it is useful to be able to visualize z-scores as locations in a distribution (see Figure 5.2 in the text). Remember, z = 0 is in the center (at the mean), and the extreme tails correspond to z-scores of approximately -2.00 on the left and +2.00 on the right. Although more extreme z-score values are possible, most of the distribution is contained between z = -2.00 and z = +2.00.

The fact that z-scores identify exact locations within a distribution means that z-scores can be used as descriptive statistics and as inferential statistics. As descriptive statistics, z-scores describe exactly where each individual is located. As inferential statistics, z-scores determine whether a specific sample is representative of its population, or is extreme and unrepresentative. For example, a sample with a z-score near zero is a central, typical sample located near the population mean. On the other hand, a sample with a z-score value beyond 2.00 (or -2.00) would be considered an extreme or unusual sample, much different from the population mean.

z-SCORES AND STANDARDIZED DISTRIBUTIONS

When an entire distribution of X values is transformed into z-scores, the resulting distribution of z-scores will always have a mean of zero and a standard deviation of one. The transformation does not change the shape of the original distribution and it does not change the location of any individual score relative to others in the distribution.

The advantage of standardizing distributions is that two (or more) different distributions can be made the same. For example, one distribution has $\mu = 100$ and $\sigma = 10$, and another distribution has $\mu = 40$ and $\sigma = 6$. When these distribution are transformed to z-scores, both will have $\mu = 0$ and $\sigma = 1$. Because z-score distributions all have the same mean and standard deviation, individual scores from different distributions can be directly compared. A z-score of +1.00 specifies the same location in all z-score distributions.

Although transforming X values into z-scores creates a standardized distribution, many people find z-scores burdensome because they consist of many decimal values and negative numbers. Therefore, it is often more convenient to standardize a distribution into numerical values that are simpler than z-scores. To create a simpler standardized distribution, you first select the mean and standard deviation that you would like for the new distribution. Then, z-scores are used to identify each individual's position in the original distribution and to compute the individual's position in the new distribution. Suppose, for example, that you want to standardize a distribution so that the new mean is $\mu = 50$ and the new standard deviation is $\sigma = 10$. An individual with a z-score of $z = -1.00$ in the original distribution would be assigned a score of $X = 40$ (below μ by one standard deviation) in the standardized distribution. Repeating this process for each individual score allows you to transform an entire distribution into a new, standardized distribution.

LEARNING OBJECTIVES

1. You should be able to describe and understand the purpose for z-scores.

2. You should be able to transform X values into z-scores or to transform z-scores into X values.

3. You should be able to describe the effects of standardizing a distribution by transforming the entire set of raw scores into z-scores.

4. By using z-scores you should be able to transform any set of scores into a distribution with a predetermined mean and standard deviation.

The following terms were introduced in this chapter. Define or describe each term and, where appropriate, describe how each term is related to other terms in the list.

raw score
z-score
z-score transformation
standard score
standardized distribution

NEW FORMULAS

$$z = \frac{X - \mu}{\sigma}$$

$$z\sigma = X - \mu = \text{deviation score}$$

$$X = \mu + z\sigma$$

STEP BY STEP

Changing X to z: The process of changing an X value to a z-score involves finding the precise location of X within its distribution. We will begin with a distribution with $\mu = 60$ and $\sigma = 12$. The goal is to find the z-score for X = 75.

Step 1:   First determine whether X is above or below the mean. This will determine the sign of the z-score. For our example, X is above μ so the z-score will be positive.

Step 2:   Next, find the distance between X and μ. For our example,

$$X - \mu = 75 - 60 = 15 \text{ points}$$

Note: Steps 1 and 2 simply determine a deviation score (sign and magnitude). If you are using the z-score formula, these two steps correspond to the numerator of the equation.

Step 3:   Convert the distance from Step 2 into standard deviation units. In the z-score equation, this step corresponds to dividing by σ. For this example,

$$15/12 = 1.25$$

If you are using the z-score definition (rather than the formula), you simply compare the magnitude of the distance (Step 2) with the magnitude of the standard deviation. For this example, our distance of 15 points is equal to one standard deviation plus 3 more points. The extra 3 points are equal to one-quarter of a standard deviation, so the total distance is one and one-quarter standard deviations.

Step 4:   Combine the sign from Step 1 with the number of standard deviations you obtained in Step 3.   For this example,

$$z = +1.25$$

Changing z to X: The process of converting a z-score into an X value corresponds to finding the score that is located at a specified position in a distribution.   Again, suppose we have a population with $\mu = 60$ and $\sigma = 12$.   What is the X value corresponding to $z = -0.50$?

Step 1:   The sign of the z-score tells whether X is above or below the mean.   For this example, the X value we want is below μ.

Step 2:   The magnitude of the z-score tells how many standard deviations there are between X and μ.   For this example, the distance is one-half a standard deviation which is $(1/2)(12) = 6$ points.

Step 3:   Starting with the value of the mean, use the direction (Step 1) and the distance (Step 2) to determine the X value.   For this example, we want to find the score that is 6 points below $\mu = 60$.   Therefore,

$$X = 60 - 6 = 54$$

HINTS AND CAUTIONS

1.   Rather than memorizing formulas for z-scores, we suggest that you rely on the definition of a z-score. Remember a z-score identifies a location by specifying

the direction from the mean (+ or -) and the distance
from the mean in terms of standard deviations.

2.   When transforming scores from X to z (or from z to X) it is
      wise to check your answer by reversing the transformation.
      For example, given a population with $\mu = 54$ and $\sigma = 4$ a
      score of X = 46 corresponds to a z-score of

$$z = \frac{X - \mu}{\sigma} = \frac{46 - 54}{4} = \frac{-8}{4} = -2.00$$

      To check this answer, convert the z-score back into an X
      value. In this case, z = -2.00 specifies a location below
      the mean by 2 standard deviations. This distance is

$$z\sigma = -2.00(4) = -8 \text{ points}$$

      With a mean of $\mu = 54$, the score must be

$$X = 54 - 8 = 46.$$

SELF-TEST AND REVIEW

1. Any score with a value less than the population mean will
have a negative z-score.   (True or False)

2.   For a population with $\mu = 50$ and $\sigma = 10$, what is the z-score
corresponding to X = 45?

3.   For a population with $\mu = 50$ and $\sigma = 10$, what is the X value
corresponding to z = 1.50?

4.   In a population with $\mu = 80$, a score of X = 88 corresponds to
z = +2.00.   What is the standard deviation for this population?

5.   In a population with $\sigma = 12$, a score of X = 64 corresponds to a z-score of -0.25.   What is the mean for this population?

6.   For a population with $\mu = 90$ and $\sigma = 25$ find the z-score corresponding to each of the following X values.

    a.   X = 95

    b.   X = 110

    c.   X = 65

    d.   X = 80

7.   For a population with $\mu = 60$ and $\sigma = 6$ find the X value corresponding to each of the following z-scores.

    a.   z = +1.50

    b.   z = -0.50

    c.   z = +2.00

    d.   z = -1/3

8.   On an exam with $\mu = 70$ and $\sigma = 10$, you have a score of X = 85.

    a.   What is your z-score on this exam?

    b.   If the instructor added 5 points to every score, what would happen to your z-score?

    c.   If the instructor multiplied every score by 2, what would happen to your z-score?

9.   For an exam with a mean score of $\mu = 80$, you have a score of X = 85.   Which value for the standard deviation would give you a better grade (a higher standing in the class), $\sigma = 5$ or $\sigma = 10$?

10.   Transforming an entire distribution of scores into z-scores will not change the shape of the distribution.   (True or False)

11.   If a population with $\mu = 60$ and $\sigma = 8$ is transformed into z-scores, then the resulting distribution of z-scores will have a mean of _____ and a standard deviation of _____.

12. A set of exam scores has $\mu = 48$ and $\sigma = 8$. The instructor would like to transform the scores into a standardized distribution with $\mu = 100$ and $\sigma = 20$. Find the transformed value for each of the following scores from the original population.

        a.   X = 48

        b.   X = 50

        c.   X = 44

        d.   X = 32

ANSWERS TO SELF-TEST

1. True

2. $z = -0.50$ (Below μ by exactly one-half of the standard deviation)

3. $X = 65$ (1.5σ = 15 points above the mean)

4. $\sigma = 4$ (8 points above the mean corresponds to 2 standard deviations above the mean)

5. $\mu = 67$ (One-quarter of a standard deviation is 3 points below the mean.)

6.   a. $z = +0.20$

     b. $z = +0.80$

     c. $z = -1.00$

     d. $z = -0.40$

7.   a. X = 69   c. X = 72

     b. X = 57   d. X = 58

8. a. Your z-score is z = 1.50.

    b. Adding 5 points to every score would increase your score and the mean by 5 points. However, your z-score (your position within the distribution) would not change.

    c. Multiplying every score by 2 will multiply the mean, the standard deviation, and your score. However, your z-score (your position within the distribution) will not change.

9. With $\sigma = 5$ your score corresponds to z = 1.00. With $\sigma = 10$, your z-score would be only z = 0.50.

10. True

11. For z-scores, $\mu = 0$ and $\sigma = 1$, always.

12. a. X = 48 corresponds to z = 0. In the new distribution this location corresponds to X = 100.

     b. X = 50 corresponds to z = +0.25 which corresponds to X = 105 in the new distribution.

     c. X = 44 corresponds to z = -.50. X = 90 in the new distribution.

     d. X = 32 corresponds to z = -2.00. X = 60 in the new distribution.

CHAPTER 6

PROBABILITY

CHAPTER SUMMARY

In this chapter we introduce the concept of probability as a method for measuring and quantifying the likelihood of obtaining a specific sample from a specific population. We define probability as a fraction or a proportion. In particular, the probability of any specific outcome is determined by a ratio comparing the frequency of occurrence for that outcome relative to the total number of possible outcomes. Whenever the scores in a population are variable it is impossible to predict with perfect accuracy exactly which score or scores will be obtained when you take a sample from the population. In this situation researchers rely on probability to determine the relative likelihood for specific samples. Thus, although a researcher may not be able to predict exactly which value(s) will be obtained for a sample, it is possible to determine exactly which outcomes have high probability and which have low probability.

Probability is determined by a fraction or proportion. When a population of scores is represented by a frequency distribution, probabilities can be defined by proportions of the distribution. In graphs, probability can be defined as a proportion of area under the curve. For normal distributions, proportions (probabilities) can be found in the unit normal table. Because normal distributions are common, and because all normal distributions have the same shape (same proportions), it is possible to have one table that serves for all normal distributions, as long as it is standardized to z-scores. The table can be used to find the proportion associated with a specific score or to find the score associated with a specific proportion. In either case, it is necessary to use z-scores as an intermediate step to define precise locations within the distribution.

Binomial distributions are formed by a series of observations (for example, 100 coin flips) for which there are two dichotomous outcomes (heads vs. tails). These distributions approach normality under certain conditions allowing the use of the unit normal table to find the probability of the event(s).

Probability is important because it establishes a link between samples and populations. For any known population it is possible to determine the probability of obtaining any specific sample. In later chapters we will use this link as the foundation for inferential statistics. The general goal of inferential statistics is to use the information from a sample to reach a general conclusion (inference) about an unknown population. Typically a researcher begins with a sample. If the sample has a high probability of being obtained from a specific population, then the researcher can conclude with some confidence that the sample actually came from that population. On the other hand, if the sample has a very low probability of being obtained from a specific population, then it is reasonable for the researcher to conclude that the specific population is probably not the source for the sample.

1.   Know how to determine the probability of an event.

2.   Be able to use the unit normal table to determine the
     probabilities for events that are normally distributed.

3.   Be able to use the unit normal table to find the specific
     score associated with given probabilities or proportions.

4.   Be able to find percentiles and percentile ranks for scores
     in a normal distribution.

5.   Be able to determine binomial probabilities using the normal
     approximation.

NEW TERMS AND CONCEPTS

     The following terms were introduced in this chapter. Define
or describe each term and, where appropriate, describe how each
term is related to other terms in the list.

     probability
     proportion
     random sample
     sampling with replacement
     independent events
     normal distribution
     unit normal table
     percentile
     percentile rank
     binomial distribution

$$p(A) = \frac{\text{Number of ways event A can occur}}{\text{Total number of possible outcomes}}$$

Semi-Interquartile Range $= 0.67\sigma$

$$z = \frac{X - pn}{\sqrt{npq}} \qquad \mu = pn \qquad \sigma = \sqrt{npq}$$

STEP BY STEP

Finding the probability associated with a specified score. The general process involves converting the score (X) into a z-score, then using the unit normal table to find the probability associated with the z-score. We will use the following example to look at the details of the process.

For a normal distribution with $\mu = 100$ and $\sigma = 10$, find the probability of randomly selecting a score greater than 95.

Step 1: Sketch the distribution and identify the mean and standard deviation.

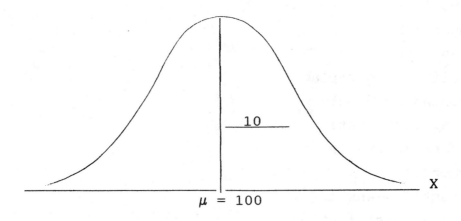

Step 2: Find the approximate location of the specified score and draw a vertical line through the distribution. For this example, X = 95 is located below the mean by roughly one-half of the standard deviation.

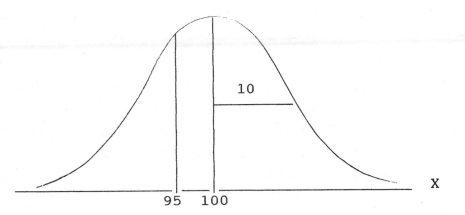

Step 3: Read the problem again to determine whether you want the proportion greater than the score (right of your line) or less than the score (left of the line). Then shade in the appropriate portion of the distribution. For this example we want the proportion consisting of scores greater than 95, so shade in the portion to the right of X = 95.

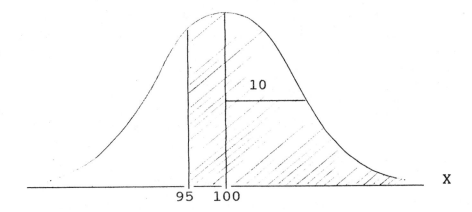

Step 4: Look at your sketch and make an estimate of the proportion that has been shaded. Remember, the mean divides the distribution in half with 50% on each side. For this example, we have shaded more than 50% of the distribution.

The shaded area appears to be about 60% or 70% of the distribution.

Step 5:   Transform the X value into a z-score. For this example, X = 95 corresponds to z = -0.50.

Step 6:   Look up the z-score value in the unit normal table. (Ignore the + or - sign.) Find the two proportions in the table that are associated with your z-score and write these two proportions in the appropriate places on your figure.   Remember, column B gives the proportion in the body of the distribution, and column C gives the area in the tail beyond z.

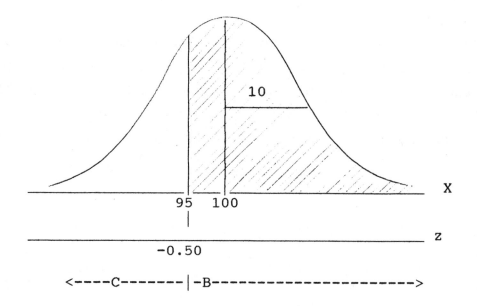

Step 7:   You must indentify the column from the table that corresponds with the shaded area of your figure. For this example, the column B proportion, 0.6915, corresponds the shaded area.

Step 8: Compare your final answer with the estimate you made in Step 4. If your answer is not in agreement with your preliminary estimate, re-work the problem.

HINTS AND CAUTIONS

1. In using probability, you should be comfortable in converting fractions into decimals or percentages. These values all represent ways of expressing portions of the whole. If you have difficulty with fractions or decimals, review the section on proportions in the math review appendix of your textbook.

2. It usually helps to restate a probability problem as a question about proportion. For example, the problem, "What is the probability of selecting an ace from a deck of cards?" becomes, "What proportion of the deck is composed of aces?"

3. When using the unit normal table to answer probability questions, you should always start by sketching a normal distribution and shading in the area of the distribution for which you need a proportion.

4. When you are computing probabilities for a binomial distribution remember to use the real limits for each score. For example, a score of X = 18 actually corresponds to an interval from 17.5 to 18.5. Also, scores greater than 18 begin at the upper real limit of 18.5.

1.   If a situation has several possible outcomes, A, B, C, D, etc., what is the definition of the probability that event A will occur?

2.   Sampling with replacement is less important when the population size is small. (True or False)

3.   The definition of probability requires random sampling. Identify the two requirements that must be met for random sampling.

4.   A container has 4 red marbles and 5 blue marbles. If one marble is selected randomly, then the probability of obtaining a red marble is 4/5 or 0.80. (True or False)

5.   In a binomial distribution, μ is
         a. pq   b. $\sqrt{npq}$ c. Xp   d. pn

6.   Assume a normal distribution for each question.
         a. What is the probability of obtaining a z-score greater than 1.25?
         b. What is the probability of obtaining a z-score less than 0.50?
         c. What proportion of the distribution consists of z-scores greater than -1.00?
         d. $p(z > 2.00) = $?
         e. $p(z < -.50) = $?

7.   Find the z-score that separates a normal distribution into the following two portions:
         a. separate the lowest 75% from the highest 25%
         b. separate the lowest 90% from the highest 10%

    c.   separate the lowest 35% from the highest 65%

    d.   separate the lowest 42% from the highest 58%

8.   Find the following probabilities for a normal distribution with $\mu = 80$ and $\sigma = 12$.

    a. $p(X > 86)$

    b. $p(X > 77)$

    c. $p(X < 95)$

    d. $p(X < 68)$

9.   For a normal distribution with $\mu = 80$ and $\sigma = 12$, find the X value associated with each of the following proportions:

    a. What X value separates the distribution into the top 40% versus the bottom 60%?

    b. What is the minimum X value needed to be in the top 25% of the distribution?

    c. What X value separates the top 60% from the bottom 40% of the distribution?

10. Find the following:

    a. For a normal distribution with $\mu = 60$ and $\sigma = 5$, what is the probability of randomly selecting a score between 61 and 65?

    b. For a normal distribution with $\mu = 60$ and $\sigma = 5$, what is the probability of randomly selecting a score between 57 and 62?

11. For this year's migration south, approximately 3 times as many mallards (q) are in any flyway than Canada geese (p). A sample of n = 100 migrants from this flyway took a rest in your farm pond. What is the probability that you would observe 32 or more ($X \geq 32$) Canada Geese in your pond?

12. Probability values are always between 0.0 and 1.0. (True or False)

13.   The unit normal table answers questions about proportions, not probability. (True or False)

14.   If a shaded area of the distribution has 22% of the scores, then the remaining part of the distribution consists of __???__ .

1.   The probability of event A is defined as a proportion:

$$p(A) \ = \ \frac{\text{number of ways event A can occur}}{\text{total number of possible outcomes}}$$

2.   False. Replacement becomes less important when populations are extraordinarily large.

3.   The two requirements for a random sample are:
a. Every individual in the population has an equal probability of being selected.
b. If more than one individual is selected, the probability of being chosen is unchanged after each selection is made.

4.   False. $p(red) = 4/9 = 0.44$

5.   choice d

6   a. $p(z > 1.25)$ = 0.1056
    b. $p(z < 0.50)$ = 0.6915
    c. $p(z > -1.00)$ = 0.8413
    d. $p(z > 2.00)$ = 0.0228
    e. $p(z < -0.50)$ = 0.3085

7. a. z = 0.67   c. z = -0.39
    b. z = 1.28   d. z = -0.20

8. a. z = 0.50 and p = 0.3085
    b. z = -0.25 and p = 0.5987
    c. z = 1.25 and p = 0.8944
    d. z = -1.00 and p = 0.1587

9. a. z = 0.25 and X = 83
    b. z = 0.67 and X = 88.04
    c. z = -0.25 and X = 77

10. a. The z-scores are 0.20 and 1.00, and p = 0.2620
    b. The z-scores are -.60 and 0.40, and p = 0.3811

11. μ = pn = 0.25(100) = 25, σ = 4.33, for X use 31.5, z = 1.50,
    p(X $\geq$ 32) = 0.0668 or 6.68%

12. True

13. False. Probability and proportion are interchangeable.

14. 78%

CHAPTER 7

THE DISTRIBUTION
OF SAMPLE MEANS

CHAPTER SUMMARY

In the previous two chapters we presented the statistical procedures for computing z-scores and finding probabilities associated with individual scores, X-values. In order to find z-scores or probabilities, the first requirement is that you must know about <u>all the possible X values</u>, that is, the entire distribution. A z-score tells where an individual X is located relative to all the other X values in the distribution. To find a probability, we simply identified a proportion of all the possible X values.

In Chapter 7 we extend the concepts of z-scores and probability to samples of more than one score. Specifically, we will compute z-scores and find probabilities for sample means. To accomplish this task, the first requirement is that you must know about <u>all the possible sample means</u>, that is, the entire distribution of $\overline{X}$'s. Once this distribution is identified, then

1. A z-score can be computed for each sample mean. The z-score tells where the specific sample mean is located relative to all the other sample means.

2. The probability associated with a specific sample mean can be defined as a proportion of all the possible sample means.

THE DISTRIBUTION OF $\overline{X}$

The <u>distribution of sample means</u> is defined as the set of means from all the possible random samples of a specific size (n) selected from a specific population. This distribution has well-defined (and predictable) characteristics that are specified in the Central Limit Theorem:

1. The mean of the distribution of sample means is called the <u>Expected Value of $\overline{X}$</u> and is always equal to the population mean μ.

2. The standard deviation of the distribution of sample means is called the <u>Standard Error of $\overline{X}$</u> and is computed by

$$\sigma_{\overline{X}} = \frac{\sigma}{\sqrt{n}}$$

3. The shape of the distribution of sample means tends to be normal. It is guaranteed to be normal if a) the population from which the samples are obtained is normal, or b) the sample size is n = 30 or more.

Within this distribution, the location of each sample mean can be specified by a z-score,

$$z = \frac{\overline{X} - \mu}{\sigma_{\overline{X}}}$$

Because the distribution of sample means tends to be normal, the z-score values can be used with the unit normal table to obtain probabilities.

The procedures for computing z-scores and finding probabilities for sample means are essentially the same as we used for individual scores (in Chapters 5 and 6). However, when you are using sample means, you must remember to consider the sample size (n) and compute the standard error ($\sigma_{\bar{X}}$) before you start any other computations. Also, you must be sure that the distribution of sample means satisfies at least one of the criteria for normal shape before you can use the unit normal table.

The concept of the distribution of sample means and its characteristics should be intuitively reasonable. First, you should realize that sample means are variable. If two (or more) samples are selected from the same population, the two samples probably will have different means. Second, although the samples will have different means, you should expect the sample means to be close to the population mean. That is, the sample means should "pile up" around μ. Thus, the distribution of sample means tends to form a normal shape with an expected value of μ. Finally, you should realize that an individual sample mean probably will not be identical to its population mean; that is, there will be some "error" between $\bar{X}$ and μ. Some sample means will be relatively close to μ and others will be relatively far away. The standard error provides a measure of the standard distance between $\bar{X}$ and μ.

THE STANDARD ERROR OF $\bar{X}$

Standard error is perhaps the single most important concept in inferential statistics. The Standard Error of $\bar{X}$ is defined as the standard deviation of the distribution of sample means and measures the standard distance between a sample mean and the population mean. Thus, the Standard Error of $\bar{X}$ provides a measure of how accurately a sample mean represents its corresponding population mean.

The magnitude of the standard error is determined by two factors: σ and n. The population standard deviation, σ, measures the standard distance between a single score (X) and the population mean. Thus, the standard deviation provides a measure of the "error" that is expected for the smallest possible sample, when n = 1. As the sample size is increased, it is reasonable to expect that the error should decrease. In simple terms, the larger the sample, the more accurately it should represent its population. The formula for standard error incorporates the intuitive relationship between standard deviation, sample size, and "error."

$$\sigma_{\overline{x}} = \frac{\sigma}{\sqrt{n}}$$

As the sample size increases, the error decreases. As the sample size decreases, the error increases. At the extreme, when n = 1, the error is equal to the standard deviation.

LEARNING OBJECTIVES

1. For any specific sampling situation, you should be able to define and describe the distribution of sample means by identifying its shape, the expected value of $\overline{X}$, and the standard error of $\overline{X}$.

2. You should be able to define and calculate the standard error of $\overline{X}$.

3.   You should be able to compute a z-score that specifies the location of a particular sample mean within the distribution of sample means.

4.   Using the distribution of sample means, you should be able to compute the probability of obtaining specific values for a sample mean obtained from a given population.

5.   You should be able to incorporate a visual presentation of standard error into a graph presenting means for a set of different samples. In addition, you should be able to use the visual presentation of standard error to help determine whether the obtained difference between two sample means reflects a "real" difference in the populations, or whether the sample mean difference is simply due to chance.

NEW TERMS AND CONCEPTS

The following terms were introduced in this chapter. Define or describe each term and, where appropriate, describe how each term is related to other terms in the list.

the distribution of sample means
sampling distribution
expected value of $\bar{X}$
standard error of $\bar{X}$
the central limit theorem

$$\sigma_{\overline{x}} = \frac{\sigma}{\sqrt{n}} \qquad \text{or} \qquad \sigma_{\overline{x}} = \sqrt{\frac{\sigma^2}{n}}$$

$$z = \frac{\overline{X} - \mu}{\sigma_{\overline{x}}}$$

STEP BY STEP

Computing Probabilities for sample means: You should recall that we have defined probability as being equivalent to proportion. Thus, the probability associated with a specific sample mean can be defined as a specific proportion of the distribution of sample means. Because the distribution of sample means tends to be normal, you can use z-scores and the unit normal table to determine proportions or probabilities. The following example demonstrates the details of this process.

For a normal population with $\mu = 60$ and $\sigma = 12$, what is the probability of selecting a random sample of $n = 36$ scores with a sample mean greater than 64? In symbols, $p(\overline{X} > 64) = $?

Step 1: Rephrase the probability question as a proportion question. For this example, "Out of all the possible sample means for $n = 36$, what proportion have values greater than 64?"

Step 2:   We are looking for a specific proportion of "all the possible sample means." The set of "all possible sample means" is the distribution of sample means. Therefore, the next step is to sketch the distribution. Show the expected value and standard error in your sketch. Caution: Be sure to use the standard error, not the standard deviation.

For this example, the distribution of sample means will have an expected value of $\mu = 60$, a standard error of $\sigma_{\bar{x}} = 12/\sqrt{36} = 2$, and it will be a normal distribution because the original population is normal (also because $n > 30$).

Caution: If the distribution of sample means is not normal, you cannot use the unit normal table to find probabilities.

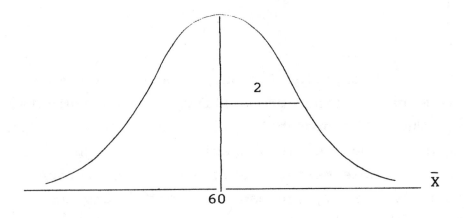

Step 3:   Find the approximate location of the specified sample mean and draw a vertical line through the distribution. For this example, $\bar{X} = 64$ is located above the mean by roughly two standard deviations.

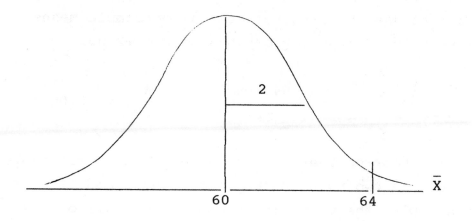

Step 4:   Determine whether the problem asked for the proportion greater than or less than the specific $\bar{X}$. Then shade in the appropriate area in your sketch.   For this example, we want the area greater than $\bar{X}$ = 64 so shade in the area on the right-hand side of the line.

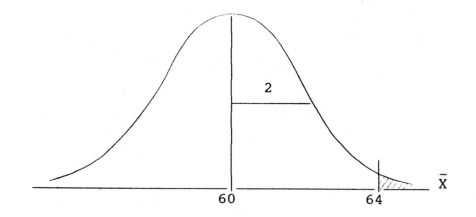

Step 5:   Look at your sketch and make a preliminary estimate of the proportion that is shaded.   For this example, we have shaded a very small part of the whole distribution, probably 5% or less.

Step 6: Compute the z-score for the specified sample mean. Be sure to use the z-score formula for sample means. For this example, $\bar{X}$ = 64 corresponds to z = +2.00.

$$z = \frac{\bar{X} - \mu}{\sigma_{\bar{x}}} = \frac{64 - 60}{2} = \frac{4}{2} = 2.00$$

Step 7: Look up the z-score in the unit normal table and find the two proportions in columns B and C. For this example, the value in column C (the tail of the distribution) corresponds exactly to the proportion we want. $p(\bar{X} > 64) = p(z > +2.00) = .0228$

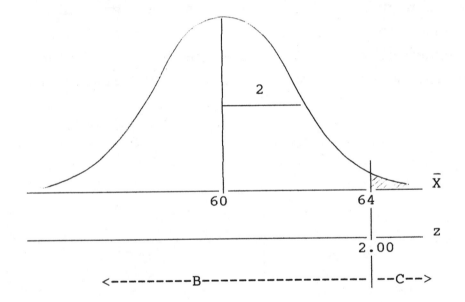

Step 8: Compare your final answer with the preliminary estimate from Step 5. Be sure that your answer is in agreement with the common-sense estimate you made earlier.

1.   Whenever you encounter a question about a sample mean you must remember to use the distribution of sample means and not the original population distribution. The population distribution contains scores (not sample means) and therefore should be used only when you have a question about an individual score (n = 1).

2.   The key to working with the distribution of sample means is the standard error of $\bar{X}$:

$$\sigma_{\bar{X}} = \frac{\sigma}{\sqrt{n}}$$

Remember, larger samples tend to be more accurate (less error) than small samples. The sample size, n, is a crucial factor in determining the error between a sample and its population.

SELF-TEST AND REVIEW

1.   Describe the characteristics (shape, central tendency, and variability) for the distribution of sample means for samples of size n = 25 selected from a normal population with μ = 90 and σ = 15.

2.   A population has μ = 40 with σ = 8. The distribution of sample means for samples of size n = 4 selected from this population would have an expected value of _____ and a standard error of _____.

3. The distribution of sample means cannot be normal unless the sample size is at least n = 30. (True or False)

4. If the distribution of sample means for n = 9 has a standard error of 6, what is the standard deviation of the population from which the samples were selected?

5. A population has a mean of μ = 75 and a standard deviation of σ = 12.

    a.   If a single score is randomly selected from this population, how close on the average should the score be to the population mean?

    b.   If a sample of n = 4 scores is randomly selected from this population, how close on the average should the sample mean be to the population mean?

    c.   If a sample of n = 36 scores is randomly selected from this population, how close on the average should the sample mean be to the population mean?

6. Each of the following samples was obtained from a population with μ = 100 and σ = 10. Find the z-score for each sample mean.

    a. $\overline{X}$ = 90 for a sample of n = 4

    b. $\overline{X}$ = 90 for a sample of n = 25

    c. $\overline{X}$ = 102 for a sample of n = 4

    d. $\overline{X}$ = 102 for a sample of n = 100

7. For a normal population with μ = 70 and σ = 9, what is the probability of obtaining a sample mean greater than 73 for a sample of n = 36 scores?

8. Given a normal population with μ = 40 and σ = 4, what is the probability of obtaining a sample mean between 39 and 41 for a sample of n = 16 scores?

9. A normal population has $\mu = 60$ and $\sigma = 10$. If you randomly select four scores from this population, what is the probability that the scores will total more than 250? (Hint: To total 250 or more, the four scores must average at last 62.5.)

ANSWERS TO SELF-TEST

1. The distribution of sample means will be normal because the population is normal. It will have a mean (expected value) of $\mu = 90$ and a standard deviation (standard error) of $15/\sqrt{25} = 3$.

2. The expected value is $\mu = 40$. The standard error is $\sigma_{\overline{x}} = 8/\sqrt{4} = 4$.

3. False. When the population distribution is normal the distribution of sample means will normal for any sample size.

4. The standard error is determined by $\sigma/\sqrt{n}$. In this case,
   $$6 = \sigma/\sqrt{9} = \sigma/3$$
   The standard deviation must be $\sigma = 18$.

5. a. The standard deviation, $\sigma = 12$, measures the standard distance between a score and the population mean.
    b. For $n = 4$, the standard error is $12/\sqrt{4} = 6$.
    c. For a sample of $n = 36$. the standard error is 2 points.

6   a. The standard error is 5, and $z = -2.00$.
    b. The standard error is 2, and $z = -5.00$.
    c. The standard error is 5, and $z = +0.40$.
    d. The standard error is 1, and $z = +2.00$.

7.   The standard error is 1.5.

$p(\bar{X} > 73) = p(z > +2.00) = 0.0228.$

8.   The standard error is 1.   The probability is

$p(-1.00 < z < +1.00) \quad = .3413 + .3413 = 0.6826.$

9.   With n = 4, the standard error is 5.

$p(\bar{X} > 62.5) = p(z > \quad +0.50) = 0.3085.$

CHAPTER 8

INTRODUCTION TO HYPOTHESIS TESTING

CHAPTER SUMMARY

Chapter 8 presents an introduction to and overview of the general procedure of hypothesis testing. Because hypothesis tests are probably the most commonly used inferential procedure, the basic concepts and terminology introduced in this chapter serve as a foundation the remaining topics in this book. In very general terms, a hypothesis test begins with a population that has unknown parameters (usually, the population mean is unknown). A random sample is then obtained from the population, and the hypothesis test provides a standardized, formal procedure for using the sample data (typically, $\bar{X}$) as the basis for evaluating hypotheses about the population.

Although hypothesis tests are used in a variety of situations, one common application is to help researchers determine whether or not a treatment has any effect on the individuals in the population. In this case, the researcher begins with a known population (before treatment). A random sample is selected and the treatment is administered to the sample. A hypothesis test is then used to make a comparison between the mean for the treated sample, and the mean for the original untreated population. If the sample statistic is substantially different from the original population parameter, we can conclude that the treatment has had an effect. However, if the sample does not look substantially different from the original population, we conclude that there does not seem to be any treatment effect.

Conclusions from hypothesis tests can get a bit tricky. Just because the sample mean (following treatment) is different from the original population mean does not necessarily indicate that the treatment has caused a change. You should recall (Chapter 7) that there usually is some discrepancy between a sample mean and a population mean simply as a result of sampling error. A hypothesis test is needed that to determine whether the obtained mean difference ($\bar{X} - \mu$) is simply due to sampling error or whether it really indicates a treatment effect.

The hypothesis-test procedure proceeds in four steps:

1. State the hypotheses and select an α level. The null hypothesis, H_o, always states the the treatment has no effect (no change, no difference). The α level establishes a criterion, or "cut-off", for making a decision about the hypotheses. The alpha level also determines the risk of a Type I error.

2. Locate the critical region. The critical region consists of outcomes that are very unlikely to occur if the null hypothesis is true. That is, the critical region is defined by sample means that are almost impossible to obtain just by chance. Their probability is $p < \alpha$. Thus, the alpha level is used to define precisely the terms "very unlikely" or "almost impossible."

3. Compute the test statistic. The test statistic (in this chapter a z-score) forms a ratio comparing the obtained difference between the sample mean and the hypothesized population mean versus the amount of difference we would expect just by chance (standard error).

4. A large value for the test statistic shows that the obtained mean difference is more than chance. If it is large enough to be in the critical region, we conclude that the difference is "significant" or that the treatment has a "significant effect." In this case we reject the null hypothesis. If the mean difference is not much larger than chance then the test statistic will have a low value. In this case, we conclude that the evidence from the sample is not sufficient, and the decision is fail to reject the null hypothesis.

LEARNING OBJECTIVES

1. Understand the logic of hypothesis testing.

2. Be able to state hypotheses and find the critical region.

3. Be able to assess sample data with a z-score and make a statistical decision about the hypotheses.

4. Know the difference between Type I and Type II errors.

5. When an experiment contains a prediction about the direction of a treatment effect, you should be able to incorporate the directional prediction into the hypothesis testing procedure and conduct a directional (one-tailed) hypothesis test.

NEW TERMS AND CONCEPTS

The following terms were introduced in Chapter 8. Define or describe each term and, where appropriate, describe how each term is related to other terms in the list.

hypothesis testing

null hypothesis H_o

alternative hypothesis H_1

Type I error

Type II error

alpha (α)

level of significance

critical region

test statistic

beta (β)

directional (one-tailed) test

power $(1 - \beta)$

NEW FORMULAS

P(Type I Error) = α

P(Type II Error) = β

Power = 1 - β

STEP BY STEP

Using a Sample to Test a Hypothesis about a Population Mean: Although the hypothesis testing procedure is presented repeatedly in the textbook, we will demonstrate one more example here. As always, we will use the standard four-step procedure. The following generic example will be used for this demonstration.

The researcher begins with a known population, in this case a normal distribution with $\mu = 50$ and $\sigma = 10$. The researcher suspects that a particular treatment will produce a change in the scores for the individuals in the population. Because it is impossible to administer the treatment to the entire population, a sample of $n = 25$ individuals is selected and the treatment is given to this sample. After receiving the treatment, the average score for this sample is $\bar{X} = 53$. Although the experiment involves only a sample, the researcher would like to use the data to make a general conclusion about how the treatment affects the entire population.

Step 1: The first step is to state the hypotheses and select an alpha level. The hypotheses always concern an unknown population. For this example, the researcher does not know what would happen if the entire population were given the treatment. Nonetheless, it is possible to state hypotheses about the effect of the treatment. Specifically, the null hypothesis says that the treatment has no effect. According to H_o, the unknown population (after treatment) is identical to the original population (before treatment). In symbols,

H_o: $\mu = 50$ (After treatment, the mean is still 50)

The alternative to the null hypothesis is that the treatment does have an effect that causes a change in the population mean. In symbols,

H_1: $\mu \neq 50$ (After treatment, the mean is different from 50)

At this time you also select the alpha-level. Traditionally, α is set at .05 or .01. If there is particular concern about a Type I error, or if a researcher desires to present overwhelming evidence for a treatment effect, a smaller alpha-level can be used (such as $\alpha = .001$).

Step 2: The next step is to locate the critical region. You should recall that the critical region is defined as the set of outcomes that are very unlikely to be obtained if the null hypothesis is true. We begin by looking at all the possible outcomes that could be obtained, then use the alpha level to determine the outcomes that are very unlikely. For this example, we look at the distribution of sample means for n = 25; that is, all the possible sample means that could be obtained if H_o were true.

The distribution of sample means will be normal because the original population is normal. The expected value is $\mu = 50$ (if H_o is true), and the standard error for n = 25 is

$$\sigma_{\bar{x}} = \frac{\sigma}{\sqrt{n}} = \frac{10}{\sqrt{25}} = \frac{10}{5} = 2$$

With $\alpha = .05$, we want to identify the most unlikely 5% of this distribution. The boundaries for the extreme 5% are determined by z-scores of $z = \pm1.96$.

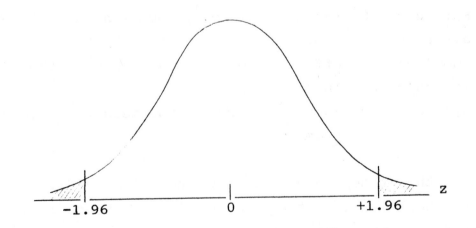

Step 3:   Obtain the Sample Data and Compute the Test Statistic.   For this example we obtained the sample mean of $\overline{X}$ = 53.   This sample mean corresponds to a z-score of,

$$z = \frac{\overline{X} - \mu}{\sigma_{\overline{x}}} = \frac{53 - 50}{2} = \frac{3}{2} = 1.50$$

Step 4:   Make Your Decision.   The z-score we obtained is not in the critical region.   This means that our sample mean, $\overline{X}$ = 53, is not an extreme or unusual value to be obtained from a population with μ = 50.   Therefore, we conclude that this sample does not provide sufficient evidence to conclude that the null hypothesis is wrong. Our statistical decision is to fail to reject H_o.   The conclusion for the experiment is that the data do not indicate that the treatment has a significant effect.

Note that the decision always consists of two parts: 1) a statistical decision about the null hypothesis, and 2) a conclusion about the outcome of the experiment.

HINTS AND CAUTIONS

1.   When using samples with n > 1, we compute a z-score for the sample mean to determine if the sample data are unlikely.   Be sure to use $\sigma_{\overline{x}}$ in the denominator, because the z-score is locating the sample mean within the distribution of sample means.

2.   When stating the hypotheses for a directional test, remember that the predicted outcome (an increase or a decrease in μ) is stated in the alternative hypothesis (H_1).

SELF-TEST AND REVIEW

1.   Statistical power will increase under which of the following conditions?
    a. small n is used
    b. df is small
    c. treatment effect is large
    d. when ß is large.

2.   Committing a type I error means you failed to reject a false null hypothesis.   (True or False)

3.   When committing a type I error, you are concluding that an effect exists, when in fact no change occurred. (True or False)

4.   Which alpha level provides the smallest chance of committing a type I error?
    a. $\alpha = .01$ b. $\alpha = .05$ c. $\alpha = .10$ d. $\alpha = .025$

5.   Identify and describe the two hypotheses that are evaluated in the hypothesis testing procedure.

6.   Throughout the book we will use the same four-step procedure for hypothesis testing.   Identify the four steps.

7.   Although a hypothesis test evaluates two hypotheses, the conclusion from the test always is stated in terms of the null hypothesis. We either "Reject H_o" or "Fail to Reject H_o". Explain why the statistical conclusion focuses on the null hypothesis.

8.   There always is some probability that a hypothesis test will lead to the wrong conclusion.
   a.   Define a Type I error.
   b.   Describe the consequences of a Type I error.
   c.   What determines the probability of a Type I error.
   d.   Define a Type II error.
   e.   Describe the consequences of a Type II error.

9.   If a sample mean falls into a critical region, then your decision should be to "fail to reject H_o." (True or False)

10.   As alpha level decreases, the size of the critical region increases. (True or False)

11.   Using words, rewrite the z-score formula to show what it does conceptually in hypothesis testing. What does the standard error measure in this formula?

12.   Reaction times for a specific task are normally distributed with $\mu = 250$ and $\sigma = 50$. A particular sample of n = 25 subjects had a mean reaction time of $\overline{X} = 274$ milliseconds. Many of the subjects later complained about distracting noises during the test session.
   a.   To assess whether their complaints are valid, determine if the sample data are significantly different from what would be expected. Use $\alpha = .05$.
   b.   Would you have reached the same conclusion if alpha had been set at .01?

13.   Scores for a standardized reading test are normally distributed with $\mu = 50$ and $\sigma = 6$ for sixth graders. A teacher suspects that his class is significantly above average for sixth grade and might need more challenging material. The class is given the standardized test, and the mean for the class of n = 16

students is $\bar{X}$ = 54.5. Are these students significantly different from the typical sixth graders? Test with alpha set at .05.

14. The typical factory worker assembles 25 skateboards per hour. The supervisor wonders if the workers will increase their production if they are paid for each skateboard made. Using a directional (one-tailed) hypothesis, state the null and alternative hypotheses in symbols. Also, which tail should be shaded?

=====

ANSWERS TO SELF-TEST

=====

1. choice c

2. False. A type II error is described.

3. True

4. choice a: alpha = .01

5. The two hypotheses are the null hypothesis (H_o) and the alternative hypothesis (H_1). The null hypothesis states that the treatment has no effect (no change, no difference), and it identifies a specific value for the unknown population mean. The alternative hypothesis states that the treatment does have an effect and the population mean is changed.

6. 1) State the hypotheses and select an alpha level.
    2) Locate the critical region.
    3) Obtain the data and compute the test statistic.
    4) Make your decision.

7.   Inferential reasoning involves using limited information to make general conclusions. In hypothesis testing we use sample data to test a hypothesis about a population. With an inferential procedure it is impossible to prove that a general conclusion is true. However, it is possible to demonstrate that a general conclusion is false or (at least) unlikely. Therefore, the null hypothesis states that the treatment has no effect, and we hope to show that this hypothesis is false or unlikely.

8.   a.   A Type I error is rejecting a true null hypothesis.
     b.   With a Type I error a researcher concludes that a treatment has an effect when in fact it does not. This can lead to a false report.
     c.   The probability of a Type I error is the alpha level selected by the researcher.
     d.   A Type II error is failing to reject a false null hypothesis.
     e.   With a Type II error a researcher concludes that the data do not provide a convincing demonstration that the treatment has any effect when in fact it does. The researcher may choose to refine and repeat the experiment.

9.   False

10. False

11. $z = \dfrac{\text{sample mean} - \text{hypothesized population mean}}{\text{standard error}}$

     The standard error measures the standard distance due to chance between a sample mean (data) and the population mean.

12. a. The critical region consists of values greater than z = +1.96 or less than z = -1.96. For this sample z = 2.40. Reject the null hypothesis and conclude that the data for this sample are significantly different from what would be expected by chance.

b. With α = .01, the critical region consists of values greater than z = +2.58 or less than -2.58. By this standard, the obtained z-score is not in the critical region, so we fail to reject H_o.

13. The null hypothesis states that these children are no different from the general population with μ = 50. In symbols, H_o: μ = 50. The critical region consists of z-scores beyond 1.96 or -1.96. The data produce a z-score of z = 3.00. Reject H_o and conclude that this sample comes from a population with a mean that is different from μ = 50.

14. H_o: $\mu \leq 25$ (being paid for each skateboard made does not increase production)

H_1: $\mu > 25$ (production increases with new pay schedule)

The right-hand tail should contain the critical region.

CHAPTER 9

INTRODUCTION TO
THE t STATISTIC

The t statistic introduced in Chapter 9 allows researchers to use sample data to test hypotheses about an unknown population mean. The particular advantage of the t statistic, compared to the z-score test in Chapter 8, is that the t statistic does not require any knowledge of the population standard deviation. Thus, the t statistic can be used to test hypotheses about a completely unknown population; that is, both μ and σ are unknown, and the only available information about the population comes from the sample. All that is required for a hypothesis test with t is a sample and a reasonable hypothesis about the population mean.

There are two general situations where this type of hypothesis test is used:

1. The t statistic is used when a researcher wants to determine whether or not a treatment causes a change in a population mean. In this case you must know the value of μ for the original, untreated population. A sample is obtained from

the population and the treatment is administered to the sample. If the resulting sample mean is significantly different from the original population mean, you can conclude that the treatment has a significant effect.

2.   Occasionally a theory or other prediction will provide a hypothesized value for an unknown population mean. A sample is then obtained from the population and the t statistic is used to compare the actual sample mean with the hypothesized population mean. A significant difference indicates that the hypothesized value for μ should be rejected.

ESTIMATING THE STANDARD ERROR BETWEEN $\bar{X}$ AND μ

Whenever a sample is obtained from a population you expect to find some discrepancy or "error" between the sample mean and the population mean. This general phenomenon is known as "sampling error." The goal for a hypothesis test is to evaluate the significance of the observed discrepancy between a sample mean and the population mean. Specifically, the hypothesis test attempts to decide between the following two alternatives:

1.   Is the discrepancy between $\bar{X}$ and μ within the margin of error? That is, is the difference between $\bar{X}$ and μ simply due to chance?

2.   Is the discrepancy between $\bar{X}$ and μ more than would be expected by chance? That is, is the sample mean significantly different from the population mean?

The critical first step for the t statistic hypothesis test is to calculate exactly how much difference between $\bar{X}$ and μ is expected by chance. However, because the population standard deviation is unknown, it is impossible to compute the standard error of $\bar{X}$ as we did with z-scores in Chapter 8. Therefore, the t statistic requires that you use the sample data to compute an estimated standard error of $\bar{X}$. This calculation defines standard error exactly as it was defined in Chapters 7 and 8, but now we must use the sample variance, s^2, in place of the unknown population variance, σ^2 (or use sample standard deviation, s, in place of the unknown population standard deviation, σ). The resulting formula for estimated standard error is

$$s_{\overline{x}} = \sqrt{\frac{s^2}{n}} \qquad \text{or} \qquad s_{\overline{x}} = \frac{s}{\sqrt{n}}$$

HYPOTHESIS TESTS WITH THE t STATISTIC

The t statistic (like the z-score) forms a ratio. The top of the ratio contains the obtained difference between the sample mean and the hypothesized population mean. The bottom of the ratio is the standard error which measures how much difference is expected by chance.

$$t = \frac{\text{obtained difference}}{\text{standard error}} = \frac{\overline{X} - \mu}{s_{\overline{x}}}$$

A large value for t (a large ratio) indicates that the obtained difference between the data and the hypothesis is greater than would be expected by chance.

You should realize that the t statistic is very similar to the z-score used for hypothesis testing in Chapter 8. In fact, you can think of the t statistic as an "estimated z-score." The estimation comes from the fact that we are using the sample variance to estimate the unknown population variance. With a large sample, the estimation is very good and the t statistic will be very similar to a z-score. With small samples, however, the t statistic will provide a relatively poor estimate of z. The value of <u>degrees of freedom</u>, df = n - 1, is used to describe how well the t statistic represents a z-score. Also, the value of df will determine how well the distribution of t approximates a normal distribution. For large values of df, the t distribution will be nearly normal, but with small values for df, the t distribution will be flatter and more spread out than a normal distribution.

To evaluate the t statistic from a hypothesis test, you must select an α level, find the value of df for the t statistic, and consult the t distribution table. If the obtained t statistic is larger than the critical value from the table, you can reject the null hypothesis. In this case, you have demonstrated that the obtained difference between the data and the hypothesis (numerator of the ratio) is significantly larger than the difference that is expected by chance (the standard error in the denominator).

The hypothesis test with a t statistic follows the same four-step procedure that was used with z-score tests (Chapter 8):

a. State the hypotheses and select a value for α.
(Note: The null hypothesis always states a specific value for μ.)

b. Locate the critical region.
(Note: You must find the value for df and use the t distribution table.)

c. Calculate the test statistic.

d. Make a decision (Either "reject" or "fail to reject" the null hypothesis).

LEARNING OBJECTIVES

1. Know when you must use the t statistic rather than a z-score for hypothesis testing.

2. Understand the concept of degrees of freedom and how it relates to the t distribution.

3. Be able to perform all of the necessary computations for hypothesis tests with the t statistic. This includes calculating the basic descriptive statistics for the sample

(mean and variance) and the estimated standard error for $\overline{X}$.

NEW TERMS AND CONCEPTS

The following terms were introduced in this chapter. Define or describe each term and, where appropriate, describe how each term is related to other terms in the list.

t statistic
estimated standard error
degrees of freedom
t distribution

NEW FORMULAS

$$t = \frac{\overline{X} - \mu}{s_{\overline{x}}}$$

$$s_{\overline{x}} = \sqrt{\frac{s^2}{n}} \qquad \text{or} \qquad s_{\overline{x}} = \frac{s}{\sqrt{n}}$$

STEP BY STEP

Hypothesis Testing with the t Statistic: The t statistic presented in this chapter is used to test a hypothesis about an unknown population mean using the data from a single sample. Calculation of the t statistic requires the sample mean $\bar{X}$ and some measure of the sample variability, usually the sample variance, s^2. A hypothesis test with the t statistic uses the same four-step procedure that we use for all hypothesis tests. However, with a t statistic, you must compute the variance (or standard deviation) for the sample of scores and you must remember to use the t distribution table to locate the critical values for the test.   We will use the following example to demonstrate the t statistic hypothesis test.

A psychologist has prepared an "Optimism Test" that is administered yearly to graduating college seniors. The test measures how each graduating class feels about its future -- the higher the score, the more optimistic the class. Last year's class had a mean score of $\mu = 56$. A sample of n = 25 seniors from this year's class produced an average score of $\bar{X} = 59$ with SS = 2400. On the basis of this sample can the psychologist conclude that this year's class has a different level of optimism than last year's class? Test at the .05 level of significance.

Note that this test will use a t statistic because the population standard deviation is not known.

Step 1:   State Hypotheses and select an alpha level. The statements of the null hypothesis and the alternative hypothesis are the same for the t statistic test as they were for the z-score test.

H_o: $\mu = 56$ (no change)

H_1: $\mu \neq 56$ (this year's mean is different)

For this example we are using $\alpha = .05$

Step 2: Locate the critical region. With a sample of n = 25, the t statistic will have df = 24. For a two-tailed test with α = .05 and df = 24, the critical t values are t = ±2.064.

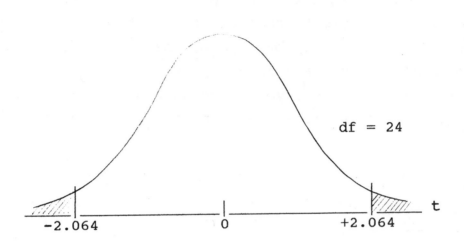

Step 3: Obtain the data and compute the test statistic: For this sample we have $\bar{X}$ = 59, SS = 2400, and n = 25. To compute the t statistic for these data, it is best to start by calculating the sample variance.

$$s^2 = \frac{SS}{n - 1} = \frac{2400}{24} = 100$$

Next, use the sample variance to compute the estimated standard error. Remember, standard error provides a measure of the standard distance between a sample mean $\bar{X}$ and its population mean μ.

$$s_{\bar{x}} = \sqrt{\frac{s^2}{n}} = \sqrt{\frac{100}{25}} = \sqrt{4} = 2$$

Finally, compute the t statistic using the hypothesized value of μ from H_o.

$$t = \frac{\overline{X} - \mu}{s_{\overline{x}}} = \frac{59 - 56}{2} = \frac{3}{2} = 1.50$$

Step 4: Make decision. The t statistic we obtained is not in the critical region. Because there is nothing unusual about this t statistic (it is the kind of value that is likely to be obtained by chance), we fail to reject H_o. These data do not provide sufficient evidence to conclude that this year's graduating class has a level of optimism that is different from last year's class.

HINTS AND CAUTIONS

1.   Students often confuse the formulas for sample variance (or standard deviation) and estimated standard error. The specific confusion is deciding when to divide by n and when to divide by n - 1.

Sample variance and standard deviation are <u>descriptive statistics</u> that were introduced in Chapter 4. You should recall that the sample mean describes the center of the distribution, and the sample standard deviation (or variance) describes how the scores are distributed around the mean. To compute the sample variance or the sample standard deviation, the correct denominator is df = n - 1.

The estimated standard error ($s_{\overline{x}}$) on the other hand, is primarily an <u>inferential statistic</u> that measures how accurately the sample mean represents its population mean. The degree of accuracy is largely determined by the size of

the sample: The bigger the sample, the smaller the error.
Thus, the magnitude of the standard error is determined by
n.   To compute the estimated standard error, the correct
denominator is n.

2.   When locating the critical region for a t test, be
      sure to consult the t distribution table, not the unit
      normal table.

=====================================
SELF-TEST AND REVIEW
=====================================

1.   To compute a t statistic, you must use the sample variance
(or standard deviation) to compute the estimated standard error
for the sample mean.   (True or False)

2.   If the sample variance increases, the estimated standard
error will also increase.   (True or False)

3.   A sample of n = 16 scores will produce a t statistic with
df = 15.   (True or False)

4.   A researcher reports a t statistic with df = 29.   How many
scores were in the sample?

5.   The distribution of t statistics tends to be flatter and more
spread out than a normal distribution.   (True or False)

6.   As the value of df increases, the t distribution tends to
become flatter and more spread out.   (True or False)

7. For a two-tailed hypothesis test with $\alpha = .05$ using a sample of n = 20 scores, the critical values for t would be t = ±2.086. (True or False)

8. A research study produces a t statistic of t = 2.22 for a sample of n = 12 scores.

    a. Is this t statistic sufficient to reject the null hypothesis using a two-tailed test with $\alpha = .05$?

    b. Is the t statistic sufficient to reject H_o using a two-tailed test with $\alpha = .01$?

9. A researcher would like to evaluate the effect of a new cold medication on reaction time. It is known that under regular circumstances the distribution of reaction times is normal with $\mu = 200$. A sample of n = 9 subjects is obtained. Each person is given the new cold medication and 30 minutes later reaction time is measured for each individual. The average reaction time for this sample is $\overline{X} = 210$, and the sample has SS = 1800. Based on these data can the researcher conclude that the cold medication has a significant effect on reaction time. Test with $\alpha = .05$.

    a. Using symbols, state the hypotheses for this test.

    b. Locate the critical region for $\alpha = .05$.

    c. Calculate the t statistic for this sample.

    d. What decision should the researcher make?

10. A researcher obtains the following sample from a population with an unknown mean and unknown standard deviation.

    Sample: 9, 13, 9, 9

    a. Compute the mean, variance, and standard deviation for the sample.

    b. Use the sample variance to compute the estimated standard error, $s_{\overline{x}}$, for the sample mean.

    c. Use the sample to test the null hypothesis that the population mean is equal to 7. Use a two-tailed test with $\alpha = .05$. (Assume the population distribution is normal).

1.   True. The t statistic is used in situations where the population variance (or standard deviation) is unknown. You must use the sample value in place of the unknown population variance.

2.   True. Standard error is directly related to sample variance.

3.   True, df = n - 1

4.   n = 30   (Remember, df = n - 1)

5.   True, especially with small samples

6.   False. As df increases, the t distribution becomes more like a normal distribution (less flat and spread out).

7.   False. With df = 19, the critical values are t = ±2.093.

8.   a.   For α = .05 and df = 11 the critical values are t = ±2.201. The obtained value, t = 2.22, is in the critical region. Reject H_o.

   b.   For α = .01 and df = 11 the critical values are t = ±3.106. The obtained t is not in the critical region. Fail to reject H_o.

9.   a. H_o: μ = 200   and H_1: $\mu \neq$ 200

   b.   With df = 8, the critical values are t = ±2.306

   c.   The sample variance is s^2 = 225, the standard error is 5, and t = 2.00.

d. Fail to reject H_o. The data are not sufficient to indicate that the medication has a significant effect on reaction time.

10. a. $\overline{X} = 10$, $s^2 = 4$, and $s = 2$
    b. The estimated standard error is 1 point.
    c. If $\mu = 7$ (from H_o), then $t = 3.00$. This is not beyond the critical value of 3.182 so the decision is to fail to reject the null hypothesis.

CHAPTER 10

HYPOTHESIS TESTS WITH TWO INDEPENDENT SAMPLES

CHAPTER SUMMARY

The independent-measures hypothesis test allows researchers to evaluate the difference between two population means using data from two separate samples, one sample representing each population. The identifying characteristic of this test is the existence of two separate or independent samples. Thus, an independent-measures design can be used to test for mean differences between two distinct populations (such as men versus women) or between two different treatment conditions (such as drug versus no-drug). The independent-measures design is used in situations where a researcher has no prior knowledge about either of the two populations (or treatments) being compared. In particular, the population means and standard deviations are all unknown. Because the population variances are not known, these values must be estimated from the sample data. Because we are trying to get the best estimate for population variance, we pool the two sample variances before computing the standard error. Then the resulting test statistic is the independent-measures t statistic.

As with all hypothesis tests, the general purpose of the independent-measures t test is to determine whether the mean difference obtained in a research study is sufficient to indicate a real mean difference between the two populations (or treatments) or whether the obtained difference is simply the result of sampling error. The hypothesis test provides a standardized, formal procedure for making this decision.

To prepare the data for analysis, the first step is to compute the sample mean and SS (or s, or s²) for each of the two samples. The hypothesis test follows the same four-step procedure outlined in Chapters 8 and 9.

1. State the hypotheses and select an α level. For the independent-measures test, H_o states that there is no difference between the two population means.

2. Locate the critical region. The critical values for the t statistic are obtained using degrees of freedom that are determined by adding together df for the first sample and df for the second sample.

3. Compute the test statistic. The t statistic for the independent-measures design has the same structure as the single sample t introduced in Chapter 9. However, in the independent-measures situation, all components of the t formula are doubled: there are two sample means, two population means, and two sources of error contributing to the standard error in the denominator.

4. Make a decision. If the t statistic ratio indicates that the obtained difference between sample means (numerator) is substantially greater than the difference expected by chance (denominator), we reject H_o and conclude that there is a real mean difference between the two populations or treatments.

1. You should be able to describe and to recognize the experimental situations where an independent-measures t statistic is appropriate for statistical inference.

2. You should be able to use the independent-measures t statistic to test hypotheses about the mean difference between two populations (or between two treatment conditions).

3. You should be able to list the assumptions that must be satisfied before an independent-measures t statistic can be computed or interpreted.

NEW TERMS AND CONCEPTS

The following terms were introduced in Chapter 10. Define or describe each term and, where appropriate, describe how each term is related to others in the list.

    independent-measures design (between-subjects design)
    pooled variance
    homogeneity of variance

$$t = \frac{(\bar{X}_1 - \bar{X}_2) - (\mu_1 - \mu_2)}{s_{\bar{X}_1 - \bar{X}_2}}$$

$$s_{\bar{X}_1 - \bar{X}_2} = \sqrt{\frac{s_P^2}{n_1} + \frac{s_P^2}{n_2}}$$

$$s_P^2 = \frac{SS_1 + SS_2}{df_1 + df_2}$$

STEP BY STEP

Hypothesis Tests with the Independent-Measures t Statistic. The independent-measures t statistic is used in situations where a researcher wants to test a hypothesis about the difference between two population means using the data from two separate (independent) samples. The test requires both sample means ($\bar{X}_1$ and $\bar{X}_2$), and some measure of the variability for each sample (usually SS). The following example will be used to demonstrate the independent-measures t hypothesis test.

A researcher wants to assess the damage to memory that is caused by chronic alcoholism. A sample of n = 10 alcoholics is obtained from a hospital treatment ward, and a control group of n = 10 non-drinkers is obtained from the hospital maintenance staff. Each person is given a brief memory test and the researcher records the memory score for each subject. The data are summarized as follows:

	Alcoholics	Control
	$\bar{X} = 43$	$\bar{X} = 57$
	SS = 400	SS = 410

Step 1: State the hypotheses and select an alpha level. As always, the null hypothesis states that there is no effect.

H_o: $(\mu_1 - \mu_2) = 0$ (no difference)

The alternative hypothesis says that there is a difference between the two population means.

H_1: $(\mu_1 - \mu_2) \neq 0$

We will use $\alpha = .05$.

Step 2:   Locate the critical region.   With n = 10 in each sample, the t statistic will have degrees of freedom equal to,

$$df = n_1 + n_2 - 2 = 18$$

Sketch the entire distribution of t statistics with df = 18 and locate the extreme 5%.   The critical values are t = ±2.101.

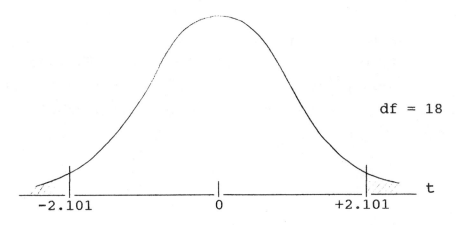

df = 18

−2.101   0   +2.101   t

Step 3: Compute the t statistic. It is easiest to begin by computing the pooled variance for the two samples.

$$s_P^2 = \frac{SS_1 + SS_2}{df_1 + df_2} = \frac{400 + 410}{9 + 9} = \frac{810}{18} = 45$$

Next, calculate the standard error for the t statistic.

$$s_{\bar{x}_1 - \bar{x}_2} = \sqrt{\frac{s_P^2}{n_1} + \frac{s_P^2}{n_2}} = \sqrt{\frac{45}{10} + \frac{45}{10}}$$

$$= \sqrt{4.5 + 4.5}$$

$$= \sqrt{9} = 3$$

Finally, use the two sample means and the standard error to calculate the t statistic.

$$t = \frac{(\bar{X}_1 - \bar{X}_2) - (\mu_1 - \mu_2)}{s_{\bar{x}_1 - \bar{x}_2}} = \frac{(43 - 57) - 0}{3}$$

$$= \frac{-14}{3} = -4.67$$

Step 4: Make decision. The t statistic for these data is in the critical region. This is a very unlikely outcome (p < .05) if H_o is true, therefore, we reject H_o. The researcher concludes that there is a significant difference between the mean memory score for chronic alcoholics and the mean score for non-drinkers.

HINTS AND CAUTIONS

1. One of the most common errors in computing the independent-measures t statistic occurs when students confuse the formulas for pooled variance and standard error. To compute the pooled variance, you combine the two samples into a single estimated variance. The formula for pooled variance uses a single fraction with SS in the numerator and df in the denominator:

$$s_P^2 = \frac{SS_1 + SS_2}{df_1 + df_2}$$

2. To compute the standard error, you add the separate errors for the two samples. In the formula for standard error these two separate sources of error appear as two separate fractions:

$$s_{\bar{x}_1 - \bar{x}_2} = \sqrt{\frac{s_P^2}{n_1} + \frac{s_P^2}{n_2}}$$

SELF-TEST AND REVIEW

1. Briefly describe what is meant by an "independent-measures" experiment.

2. The null hypothesis for an independent-measures study may be stated as H_0: $\mu_1 - \mu_2 \neq 0$. (True or False)

3. For the independent-measures t statistic, df = $n_1 + n_2 - 2$. (True or False)

4.   You will be much more likely to detect a treatment effect
when $s_{\bar{x}_1 - \bar{x}_2}$ is large. (True or False)

5.   There are two sources of error in the independent-measures
study because there are two samples representing two populations.
(True or False)

6.   To compute the independent-measures t statistic you first
must combine the two sample variances into a single value called
the pooled variance.
     a. Find the pooled variance for the following two
     samples:

               Sample 1:   n = 7 and SS = 58
               Sample 2:   n = 5 and SS = 42

     b. Find the pooled variance for the following two samples.
     (Note: When two samples are the same size, you can simply
     average the two variances. Otherwise, it is easier to
     compute SS for each sample, then use the formula for pooled
     variance.)
               Sample 1:   n = 12 and s^2 = 4
               Sample 2:   n = 10 and s^2 = 6

7.   The homogeneity assumption states that the two population
means must be equal. (True or False)

8.   A researcher would like to demonstrate how different
schedules of reinforcement can influence behavior. Two separate
groups of rats are trained to press a bar in order to receive a
food pellet. One group is trained using a fixed ratio schedule
where they receive one pellet for every 10 presses of the bar.
The second group is trained using a fixed interval schedule where
they receive one pellet for the first bar press that occurs
within a 30 second interval. Note that the second group must

wait 30 seconds before another pellet is possible no matter how many times the bar is pressed. After 4 days of training, the researcher records the response rate (number of presses per minute) for each rat. The results are summarized as follows:

Fixed Ratio	Fixed Interval
$n = 4$	$n = 8$
$\bar{X} = 30$	$\bar{X} = 18$
$SS = 90$	$SS = 150$

Do these data indicate that there is a significant difference in responding for these two reinforcement schedules? Test at the .05 level of significance.

9. A psychologist is examining the educational advantages of a preschool program. A sample of 24 fourth grade children is obtained. Half of these children had attended preschool and the others had not. The psychologist records the scholastic achievement score for each child and obtained the following data:

Preschool			No Preschool		
8	6	8	8	5	7
9	7	7	6	8	5
6	9	8	7	5	6
9	7	8	7	5	6

Do these data indicate that participation in a preschool program gives children a significant advantage in scholastic achievement? Use a one-tailed test at the .05 level.

10. Use a F-max test to determine whether or not the data from problem 9 satisfy the homogeneity of variance assumption.

11. The following data are from two separate samples. Does it appear that these two samples came from the same population or from two different populations?

   a. Use an F-max test to determine whether there is
      evidence for a significant difference between the

two population variances. Use the .05 level of significance.

b. Use an independent-measures t test to determine whether there is evidence for a significant difference between the two population means. Again, use $\alpha = .05$.

Sample 1	Sample 2
n = 10	n = 10
$\overline{X}$ = 32	$\overline{X}$ = 18
SS = 890	SS = 550

ANSWERS TO SELF-TEST

1. An independent-measures experiment uses a separate, or independent, sample for each treatment condition.

2. False. The null hypothesis states that there is no difference between the two population means. In symbols, H_o: $(\mu_1 - \mu_2) = 0$

3. True

4. False. A large value for standard error will result in a small value for t.

5. True

6. a. pooled variance = 100/10 = 10

    b. For sample 1, SS = 44. For sample 2, SS = 54. The pooled variance is 98/20 = 4.9.

7. False. The homogeneity of variance assumption states that the two populations from which the samples are obtained have the same variance. In symbols, $\sigma^2_1 = \sigma^2_2$.

8. With df = 10, the critical t values are t = ±2.228. These data have a pooled variance of 24 and produce a t statistic of t = 4.00. Reject H_o. The data provide sufficient evidence to conclude that there is a significant difference between the two schedules.

9. The psychologist expects the preschool children (sample 1) to have higher scores, so the hypotheses are,

$$H_o: \quad (\mu_1 - \mu_2) \le 0 \quad \text{(preschool is not higher)}$$
$$H_1: \quad (\mu_1 - \mu_2) > 0 \quad \text{(preschool is higher)}$$

The critical region consists of t values greater than t = +1.717. For these data $\bar{X}_1 = 7.67$ and $\bar{X}_2 = 6.25$, $SS_1 = 12.67$ and $SS_2 = 14.25$. The pooled variance is 1.22, and t = 3.16. Reject H_o and conclude that the preschool children score significantly higher on the scholastic achievement test.

10. The two sample variances are 1.15 and 1.30. F-max = 1.13. The critical value is 3.28 (using df = 12), so we fail to reject H_o. There is no significant difference between the two sample variances.

11. a. For these data, F-max = 1.62. The critical value for α = .05 is 4.03. Fail to reject H_o. There is insufficient evidence to conclude that the two population variances are different.

   b. For these data the pooled variance is 80 and the t statistic is t = 14/4 = 3.50. Reject H_o and conclude that the two population means are different.

CHAPTER 11

HYPOTHESIS TESTS WITH RELATED SAMPLES

CHAPTER SUMMARY

In a <u>repeated-measures design</u>, a single sample of individuals is obtained and each individual is measured in both of the treatment conditions being compared. Thus, the data consist of two scores for each individual. In a similar design, called a <u>matched-subjects design</u>, each individual in one treatment condition is matched one-to-one with a corresponding individual in the second treatment. The matching is accomplished by selecting pairs of subjects so that the two subjects in each pair have identical (or nearly identical) scores on the variable that is being used for matching. Thus, the data consist of pairs of scores with each pair corresponding to a matched set of two "identical" subjects.

HYPOTHESIS TESTS WITH THE REPEATED-MEASURES t

The repeated-measures t statistic allows researchers to test hypothesis about the population mean difference between two treatment conditions using sample data from either a repeated-

measures or a matched-subjects research study. The key element
with either type of research design is that the sample of
individuals in one treatment condition is matched exactly, one-
to-one, with the sample of individuals in the second treatment
condition. Thus, the scores in the first treatment are
statistically related to the scores in the second treatment. In
this situation it is possible to compute a <u>difference score</u> for
each individual (or matched pair):

$$\text{difference score} \;=\; D \;=\; X_2 - X_1$$

The sample of difference scores is then used to test hypotheses
about the population of difference scores. The null hypothesis
states that the population of difference scores has a mean of
zero,

$$H_0: \quad \mu_D = 0$$

In words, the null hypothesis says that there is no consistent or
systematic difference between the two treatment conditions.
According to the null hypothesis, any non-zero mean difference
that is observed for a sample is simply the result of sampling
error. (Note: The null hypothesis does not claim that each
individual subject will have a zero difference between
treatments. Some subjects will show a positive change from one
treatment to the other, and some subjects will show a negative
change. On average, however, the entire population will show a
mean difference of zero.)

The alternative hypothesis states that there is a real, non-
zero difference between the treatments:

$$H_1: \quad \mu_D \neq 0$$

According to the alternative hypothesis, the sample mean
difference obtained in the research study is a reflection of the
true mean difference that exists in the population.

The repeated-measures t statistic forms a ratio with exactly the same structure as the single-sample t statistic presented in Chapter 9. The numerator of the t statistic measures the difference between the sample mean and the hypothesized population mean. The bottom of the ratio is the standard error, which measures how much difference is expected by chance.

$$t = \frac{\text{obtained difference}}{\text{standard error}} = \frac{\bar{D} - \mu_D}{s_{\bar{D}}}$$

For the repeated-measures t statistic, all calculations are done with the sample of difference scores. The mean for the sample appears in the numerator of the t statistic and the variance of the difference scores is used to compute the standard error in the denominator. As usual, the standard error is computed by

$$s_{\bar{D}} = \sqrt{\frac{s^2}{n}} \qquad \text{or} \qquad s_{\bar{D}} = \frac{s}{\sqrt{n}}$$

VARIANCE AND INDIVIDUAL DIFFERENCES

The first step in the calculation of the repeated-measures t statistic is to find the difference score for each subject. This simple process has two very important consequences.

1. First, the D score for each subject provides an indication of how much difference there is between the two treatments. If all of the subjects show roughly the same D scores, then you can conclude that there appears to be a consistent, systematic difference between the two treatments. You should also note that when all the D scores are similar, the variance of the D scores will be small, which means that the standard error will be small and the t statistic is more likely to be significant.

2. Also, you should note that the process of subtracting to obtain the D scores removes the individual differences from the data. That is, the initial differences in performance from one subject to another are eliminated. Removing individual differences also tends to reduce the variance, which creates a smaller standard error and increases the likelihood of a significant t statistic.

The following data demonstrate these points:

Subject	X_1	X_2	D
A	9	16	7
B	25	28	3
C	31	36	5
D	58	61	3
E	72	79	7

First, notice that all of the subjects show an increase of roughly 5 points when they move from treatment 1 to treatment 2. Because the treatment difference is very consistent, the D scores are all clustered close together will produce a very small value for s^2. This means that the standard error in the bottom of the t statistic will be very small.

Second, notice that the original data show big differences from one subject to another. For example, subject B has scores in the 20's and subject E has scores in the 70's. However, these big individual differences are eliminated when the difference scores are calculated. Because the individual differences are removed, the D scores are usually much less variable that the original scores. Again, a smaller variance will produce a smaller standard error, which will increase the likelihood of a significant t statistic.

1. Know the difference between independent-measures and related-samples experimental designs.

2. Know the difference between a repeated-measures and a matched-subjects experimental design.

3. Be able to perform the computations for the related-samples t test.

4. Understand the advantages and disadvantages of the repeated-measures design and when this type of study is appropriate.

===================
NEW TERMS AND CONCEPTS
===================

The following terms were introduced in this chapter. Define or describe each term and, where appropriate, describe how each term is related to other terms in the list.

repeated-measures design

matched-samples design

related-samples t statistic

difference scores

estimated standard error of $\bar{D}$

individual differences

$$D = X_2 - X_1$$

$$t = \frac{\bar{D} - \mu_D}{s_{\bar{D}}}$$

$$s_{\bar{D}} = \sqrt{\frac{s^2}{n}} \qquad \text{or} \qquad s_{\bar{D}} = \frac{s}{\sqrt{n}}$$

═════════════
STEP BY STEP
═════════════

Hypothesis Testing with the related-samples t. The related-samples t statistic is used to test for a mean difference (μ_D) between two treatment conditions using data from a single sample of subjects where each individual is measured first in one treatment condition and then in the second condition. This test statistic also is used for matched-subjects designs which consists of two samples with the subjects in one sample matched one-to-one with the subjects in the second sample. Often, a repeated-measures experiment consists of a "before/after" design where each subject is measured before treatment and then again after treatment. The following example will be used to demonstrate the related-samples t test.

A researcher would like to determine whether a particular treatment has an effect on performance scores. A sample of n = 16 subjects is selected. Each subject is measured before receiving the treatment and again after treatment. The researcher records the difference between the two scores for each subject. The difference scores averaged $\bar{D}$ = -6 with SS = 960.

Step 1: State the hypotheses and select an alpha level. In the experiment the treatment was given to a sample, but the researcher wants to determine whether the treatment has any effect for the general population. As always, the null hypothesis says that there is no effect.

H$_o$: μ_D = 0 (on average, the before/after difference for the population is zero)

The alternative hypothesis states that the treatment does produce a difference.

H$_1$: $\mu_D \neq$ 0

We will use α = .05.

Step 2: Locate the critical region. With a sample of n = 16 the related-samples t statistic will have df = 15. Sketch the distribution of t statistics with df = 15 and locate the extreme 5% of the distribution. The critical boundaries are t = ±2.131.

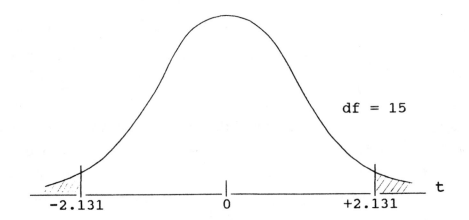

Step 3: Calculate the test statistic. As with all t statistics, it is easier to begin the calculation with the denominator of the t formula. For this example, the variance for the difference scores is

$$s^2 = \frac{SS}{n-1} = \frac{960}{15} = 64$$

With a sample of n = 16, the standard error is

$$s_{\bar{D}} = \sqrt{\frac{s^2}{n}} = \sqrt{\frac{64}{16}} = \frac{8}{4} = 2$$

Finally, substitute the sample mean difference and the standard error in the t formula,

$$t = \frac{\bar{D} - \mu_D}{s_{\bar{D}}} = \frac{-6 - 0}{2} = \frac{-6}{2} = -3.00$$

Step 4: Make Decision. The t statistic is in the critical region. This is a very unlikely value for t if H_o is true. Therefore, we reject H_o. The researcher concludes that the treatment does have a significant effect on performance scores.

HINTS AND CAUTIONS

1.   It is important to remember that the related-samples analysis is based on difference scores (D scores). Therefore, the computations of s^2 and $s_{\bar{D}}$ are based on the sample of D scores.

2. When calculating the difference scores, be sure all
   of them are obtained by subtracting in the same direction.
   That is, you may use either 1st - 2nd, or 2nd - 1st as long
   as the same method is used throughout.

=========================
SELF-TEST AND REVIEW
=========================

1. A researcher would like to conduct a study comparing two
treatment conditions with 30 individuals measured in each
treatment.
   a. How many subjects would be needed if the researcher
      uses an independent-measures design?
   b. How many subjects would be needed if the researcher
      uses a repeated-measures design?
   c. How many subjects would be needed if the researcher
      uses a matched-subjects design?

2. Calculate the difference scores and the mean difference,
D, for the following sample.

Subject	1st	2nd	D
#1	8	10	
#2	6	12	
#3	10	7	
#4	9	17	
#5	7	14	

3. A researcher selects a sample of $n = 10$ individuals and
measures each person's performance in two treatment conditions.
If the results of this experiment are evaluated using a
related-samples t, what would be the df for the t statistic?

4. A researcher reports a t statistic with df = 19 for a repeated-measures experiment comparing two treatment conditions. How many subjects participated in this experiment?

5. A repeated-measures test usually is more likely to detect a real treatment effect than an independent-measures test because the repeated-measures design reduces the standard error by removing individual differences. (True or False)

6. As the variance of the difference scores increases, the value of the t statistic decreases (closer to zero). (True or False)

7. As the size of the difference scores increases, the value of the t statistic decreases (closer to zero). (True or False)

8. A researcher would like to test the effect of a new diet drug on the activity level of animals. A sample of n = 16 rats is obtained and each rat's activity level is measured on an exercise wheel for one hour prior to receiving the drug. Thirty minutes after receiving the drug, each rat is again tested on the activity wheel. The data show that the rats increased their activity by an average of $\bar{D}$ = 21 revolutions with SS = 6000 after receiving the drug. Do these data indicate that the drug had a significant effect on activity. Test at the .05 level.
     a.   Using symbols, state the hypotheses for this test.
     b.   Locate the critical region for α = .05.
     c.   Compute the t statistic for these data.
     d.   What decision should the researcher make.

9. An educator would like to assess the effectiveness of a new instructional program for reading. The control group consists of 4 second-grade students who are provided with the traditional instruction used at the school. Another sample of 4 second-graders receives the experimental instruction.

The subjects in the experimental group are matched one-to-one with the subjects in the control group based on their reading achievement test scores from the previous year. After six months, both groups are tested with a standard reading exam. The data are as follows:

Matched Pair	Control	Experimental
A	10	12
B	15	25
C	13	15
D	18	20

On the basis of these data can the educator conclude that the special program has a significant effect on reading scores? Test at the .05 level.

ANSWERS TO SELF-TEST

1. a. An independent-measures design would require two separate samples of n = 30 for a total of 60 subjects.
    b. A repeated-measures design would require only one sample of n = 30 subjects.
    c. A matched-subjects design would require two matched samples of n = 30 for a total of 60 subjects.

2.

Subject	1st	2nd	D	
#1	8	10	+2	
#2	6	12	+6	$\Sigma D = 20$
#3	10	7	-3	
#4	9	17	+8	$\bar{D} = 20/5 = 4$
#5	7	14	+7	

3. df = n - 1 = 9

4. n = 20 subjects (df = n - 1)

5. True

6. True. Increased variance will produce an increased standard error and result in a smaller value for t.

7. False. The larger the mean difference, the larger the value for t.

8. a. H_o: $\mu_D = 0$ (no effect). H_1: $\mu_D \neq 0$
    b. With df = 15 and α = .05, the critical value are t = ±2.131
    c. The sample variance is $s^2 = 400$, the standard error is 5 points, and t(15) = 4.2.
    d. Reject the null hypothesis. The diet drug has a significant effect on activity.

9. The null hypothesis states that there is no difference between the traditional program and the new program. With df = 3, the critical t value is 3.182. For these data, $\bar{D}$ = 4, SS = 48, and t = 2. Fail to reject H_o.

CHAPTER 12

ESTIMATION

Chapter 12 introduces the inferential process of estimation. In general terms, estimation uses a sample statistic as the basis for estimating the value of the corresponding population parameter. Although estimation and hypothesis testing are similar in many respects, they are complementary inferential processes. A hypothesis test is used to determine whether or not a treatment has an effect, while estimation is used to determine how much effect.

This complementary nature occurs because estimation is often used after a hypothesis test that resulted in rejecting the null hypothesis. In this situation, the hypothesis test has established that a treatment effect exists and the next logical step is to determine how much effect. It is also common to use estimation in situations where a researcher simply wants to learn about an unknown population. In this case, a sample is selected from the population and the sample data are then used to estimate the population the population parameters.

You should keep in mind that even though estimation and hypothesis testing are inferential procedures, these two

techniques differ in terms of the type of question they address.
A hypothesis test, for example, addresses the somewhat academic
question concerning the existence of a treatment effect.
Estimation, on the other hand, is directed toward the more
practical question of how much effect. When a hypothesis test
established that a treatment has a "statistically significant"
effect, it simply means that the observed treatment effect is
greater than would be expected by chance variation. You should
note that this conclusion does not necessarily imply anything
about the actual size of the effect. A new medication, for
example, may consistently and reliably reduce blood pressure by
1%. Although this effect may be statistically significant, it
may have little or no practical significance for treating high
blood pressure. By using estimation, researchers are able to
determine the magnitude of the treatment effect. Often the size
of a treatment effect is more important than the mere existence
of an effect, especially when the treatment is being considered
for practical application.

There is an estimation procedure that accompanies each of
the four hypothesis tests presented in the preceding four
chapters. The estimation process begins with the same z or t
statistic that is used for the corresponding hypothesis test.
These all have the same conceptual structure:

$$z \text{ or } t = \frac{\text{sample statistic - unknown parameter}}{\text{standard error}}$$

The basic estimation formula is obtained by solving this equation
for the unknown parameter:

$$\text{unknown parameter} = \text{statistic} \pm (z \text{ or } t)(\text{standard error})$$

To use this equation, you first must obtain a value for z or t by
estimating the location of the data within the appropriate

distribution. The estimated value for z or t is then substituted in the equation along with the known values for the statistic and the standard error. Then the equation is solved for the unknown parameter. For a point estimate, a value of zero is used for z or t, yielding a single value for your estimate of the unknown population parameter. For interval estimates, you first select a level of confidence and then find the appropriate interval range of z or t values in the unit normal table and t distribution table, respectively.

===

LEARNING OBJECTIVES

===

1.   You should be able to use sample data to make a point estimate or an interval estimate of an unknown population mean using either a z-score (when σ is known) or a t statistic (when σ is unknown).

2.   You should be able to make a point estimate or an interval estimate of a population mean difference using sample data from an independent-measures experiment or from a related-samples experiment.

3.   You should understand how the size of a sample influences the width of a confidence interval.

4.   You should understand how the level of confidence (the % confidence) influences the width of a confidence interval.

NEW TERMS AND CONCEPTS

The following terms were introduced in this chapter. Define or describe each term and, where appropriate, describe how each term is related to other terms in the list.

estimation
point estimate
interval estimate (confidence interval)

NEW FORMULAS

$$\mu = \bar{X} \pm z\sigma_{\bar{x}}$$

$$\mu = \bar{X} \pm ts_{\bar{x}}$$

$$\mu_D = \bar{D} \pm ts_{\bar{D}}$$

$$(\mu_1 - \mu_2) = (\bar{X}_1 - \bar{X}_2) \pm ts_{\bar{x}_1 - \bar{x}_2}$$

STEP BY STEP

The following examples will be used to demonstrate the step-by-step procedures for estimation with z-scores and with the t statistic.

A researcher begins with a normal population with μ = 60 and σ = 8. The researcher is evaluating a specific treatment that is expected to increase scores. The treatment is administered to a sample of n = 16 individuals, and the mean for the treated sample is $\overline{X}$ = 66.

Estimation with z-scores: For our example, the researcher does not know the mean for the population after treatment. The researcher expects that the treated population will have a mean greater than 60 because the treatment is expected to increase scores. However, the only available information comes from the sample mean which can be used to estimate the mean for the unknown population. Because the population standard deviation is known, the z-score formula for estimation is appropriate.

Step 1: Begin with the basic formula for estimation. Remember, this is simply the regular z-score formula that has been solved for μ.

$$\mu = \overline{X} \pm z\sigma_{\overline{X}}$$

Step 2: Determine whether you are computing a point estimate or an interval estimate. If you want an interval, you must specify a level of confidence. We will compute a point estimate and a 90% confidence interval for the unknown population mean.

Step 3: Find the appropriate z-score values to substitute in the equation. For a point estimate, always use z = 0 which is the point in the exact middle of the distribution. For a 90% confidence interval, we want the z-score values that form the boundaries for the middle 90% of the distribution. These values are obtained from the unit normal table. You should find that 90% of a

normal distribution is contained between z = +1.65 and
z = -1.65.

Step 4:   Compute $\bar{X}$ and $\sigma_{\bar{x}}$ from the sample data.   For
this example we are given $\bar{X}$ = 66 and you can compute
$$\sigma_{\bar{x}} \;=\; \sigma/\sqrt{n} \;=\; 8/\sqrt{16} \;=\; 8/4 \;=\; 2$$

Step 5:   Substitute the appropriate values in the
estimation   equation.

point estimate	interval estimate
$\mu \;=\;$ 66 ± 0	$\mu \;=\;$ 66 ± (1.65)(2)
$\mu \;=\;$ 66	$\mu \;=\;$ 66 ± 3.30
	Estimate μ between
	62.70 and 69.30

Estimation with the t statistic: For our example, the population
standard deviation was given.   But if the value for σ is unknown,
it is still possible to estimate the mean for the population
after treatment.   Suppose that our researcher simply knows that
the original population mean is μ = 60 and that the treatment is
expected to produce an increase in the scores.   The treatment is
administered to a sample of n = 16 individuals and produces a
sample mean of $\bar{X}$ = 66 with SS = 1215.   Because the population
standard deviation is not known, the t statistic formula for
estimation is appropriate.

Step 1:   Begin with the basic formula for estimation.
Again, this is simply the regular t formula that has been
solved for μ.
$$\mu \;=\; \bar{X} \pm t s_{\bar{x}}$$

Step 2: Determine whether you are computing a point estimate or an interval estimate. If you want an interval, you must specify a level of confidence. We will compute a point estimate and a 90% confidence interval for the unknown population mean.

Step 3: Find the appropriate t values to substitute in the equation. For a point estimate, always use t = 0 which is the point in the exact middle of the distribution. For a 90% confidence interval, we want the t values that form the boundaries for the middle 90% of the distribution. These values are obtained from the t distribution table using df = n − 1 = 15. You should find that with df = 15, 90% of the t distribution is contained between t = +1.753 and t = −1.753.

Step 4: Compute $\bar{X}$ and $s_{\bar{x}}$ from the sample data. For this example we are given $\bar{X} = 66$ and you can compute

$$s^2 = \frac{SS}{n-1} = \frac{1215}{15} = 81$$

$$s_{\bar{x}} = \sqrt{\frac{s^2}{n}} = \sqrt{\frac{81}{16}} = \frac{9}{4} = 2.25$$

Step 5: Substitute the appropriate values in the estimation equation.

point estimate	interval estimate
$\mu = 66 \pm 0$	$\mu = 66 \pm (1.753)(2.25)$
$\mu = 66$	
	$\mu = 66 \pm 3.94$
	Estimate μ between
	62.06 and 69.94

HINTS AND CAUTIONS

1. When computing a confidence interval after a hypothesis test, many students incorrectly take the z-score or t value that was computed in the hypothesis test and use this value in the estimation equation. Remember, the z-score or t value in the estimation equation is determined by the level of confidence. For example, an 80% confidence interval with z-scores always uses $z = \pm1.28$ no matter what z-score was obtained from the hypothesis test.

2. When trying to locate the appropriate t value for a confidence interval, remember to use the "proportion in two tails" column of the t table. For an 80% confidence interval, for example, there would be 20% of the distribution left in the two tails and you should use the .20 column for two tails of the distribution.

SELF-TEST AND REVIEW

1. All other things being equal, if standard error is small, then the confidence interval will be small. (True or False)

2. To gain precision in an estimate, you must lose some confidence. (True or False)

3. It is best to use the 90% confidence level when testing a hypothesis. (True or False)

4. Holding everything else constant, as df increases, the width of the confidence interval will decrease. (True or False)

5. All other things being constant, which confidence level will provide the smallest width?
     a. 99%   b. 90%   c. 75%   d. 60%

6. Which of the following is <u>not</u> needed when determining a confidence interval estimate of μ_D?
     a. SS   b. n   c. $s_{\bar{X} - \bar{X}}$ d. $\bar{D}$

7. The process of using sample data to estimate population parameters is known as estimation. In this chapter we examined the procedures for using sample means as the basis for estimating unknown population means. Population means can be estimated using either a point estimate or an interval estimate.
    a. Define these two types of estimation.
    b. Describe point estimates and interval estimates in terms of confidence and precision.

8. Estimation often is used after a hypothesis test. Although these two inferential techniques involve many of the same calculations, they are intended to answer different questions.
    a. In general terms, what information is provided by a hypothesis test and what information is provided by estimation?
    b. Explain why it would not be appropriate do use estimation after a hypothesis test where the decision was "fail to reject" the null hypothesis.

9. The procedures for estimation are based on the fact that a sample mean, on average, provides an accurate, unbiased estimate of its population mean. Thus, $\bar{X}$ is always used as the point estimate of μ, and $\bar{X}$ always forms the midpoint of a confidence

interval for μ. The width of a confidence interval is influenced by other factors.

    a.   Explain how the width of a confidence interval is related to the sample size, n.

    b.   Explain how the width of a confidence interval is related to the level of confidence (the % confidence).

10.   A sample of n = 16 scores is obtained from a normal population with σ = 12. The sample mean is $\bar{X}$ = 43.

    a.   Use these data to make a point estimate of the population mean.

    b.   Make an interval estimate of μ so that you are 90% confident that the mean is in your interval.

11.   Each year the state college accepts a group of marginally qualified students who are designated as "special admits." In the past these students have finished their first year with a mean grade point average of μ = 2.01. Last summer the college conducted a special summer program to help prepare special-admit students for their freshman year. The sample of n = 25 students in the special program completed the year with a mean grade point average of $\bar{X}$ = 2.41 with SS = 6.

    a.   Use the data to make a point estimate of the mean grade point average that would be obtained if the entire population of special-admit students went through the summer program.

    b.   Based on your answer to part a, how much effect does the summer program have on grade point average for the special-admit students?

    c.   Make an interval estimate of the population mean after the summer program so that you are 80% confident that the true mean is in your interval.

12.   A researcher studying animal learning is investigating the effectiveness of a new training procedure. Under regular

circumstances, rats require an average of $\mu = 35$ errors before they master a standard problem-solving task. The researcher tests the effectiveness of the new procedure using a sample of n = 25 rats, and obtains a sample mean of $\overline{X} = 29$ errors with SS = 2400.

    a.   Make a point estimate of the population mean number of errors using the new training procedure.

    b.   Make an interval estimate of the population mean so that you are 90% confident that the new mean is in your interval.

13.   A high school counselor has designed a three-week course to provide students with special training in study skills and note taking. To evaluate the effectiveness of this course, a sample of n = 36 sophomores is obtained. The counselor records the fall term grade average for each student. These students then take the special course before the spring term begins, and the counselor records each student's average for the spring term. On average, these students scored 8 points higher during the spring term with SS = 1260.

    a.   On the basis of these data, can the counselor conclude that the special course has a significant effect on student performance? Test at the .05 level of significance.

    b.   Use the data to make a point estimate of how much improvement results from taking the special course.

    c.   Make an interval estimate of the mean improve ment so that you are 90% confident that the true mean improvement is contained in your interval.

14.   The government has developed a pamphlet listing driving tips that are designed to promote fuel ecomony. To test the effectiveness of these tips, a sample of twenty families is obtained, all with identical cars and similar driving habits. Ten of these families are given the pamphlet and instructions to

follow the driving tips carefully. The other ten families are simply instructed to monitor their gas mileage for a two-week period. At the end of two weeks, the gas mileage figures for both groups are as follows:

Experimental Group with Pamphlet		Control Group no Pamphlet	
25.1	28.7	24.0	23.6
22.8	25.0	25.3	25.4
27.2	29.1	24.9	22.3
28.4	27.5	21.6	23.2
26.9	30.1	24.1	26.2

a. Do these data indicate that the driving tips have a significant effect on gas mileage? Test at the .05 level of significance.

b. Use the data to make a point estimate of how much improvement in gas mileage results from following the tips.

c. Use the data to construct a 90% confidence interval to estimate how much effect the driving tips have on gas mileage.

================

ANSWERS TO SELF-TEST

================

1. True. Less error will result in a narrower width.

2. True. And you can increase % confidence at the expense of the precision of your estimate.

3.   False. The percent confidence you choose for an interval estimate has nothing to do with the hypothesis test. Although similar, do not confuse confidence level with level of significance.

4.   True. With greater df, the t values will be smaller making the confidence interval narrower. Also, greater df implies a larger sample which means less error.

5.   choice d

6.   choice c

7.   a. For a point estimate, a single value is used to estimate the population mean. For an interval estimate, the population mean is estimated to be contained within a range of values.
      b. Point estimates have great precision but no confidence. Interval estimates have increased confidence but less precision.

8.   a. A hypothesis test is intended to determine whether or not a treatment effect exists. Estimation is used to determine how much effect.
      b. If the decision from the hypothesis test is "fail to reject H_o "then the data do not provide sufficient evidence to conclude that there is any treatment effect. In this case, it would not be reasonable to use estimation in an attempt to determine "how much" effect exists.

9.   a. As the sample size increases, the standard error decreases and the width of the confidence interval decreases.
      b. As the level of confidence increases the width of the confidence interval also increases.

10. a. Use $\bar{X} = 43$ as the point estimate of μ.
     b. The 90% confidence interval extends from 38.05
     to 47.95.

11. a. Use sample mean, $\bar{X} = 2.41$, as the point estimate of μ.
     b. Based on the difference between the point estimate
     (2.41) and the former mean (2.01), you can estimate that the
     summer program has the effect of increasing grade point
     average by 0.40 points.
     c. The 80% confidence interval would be $\mu = 2.41 \pm$
     (1.318)(0.10), which gives an interval extending from 2.5418
     to 2.2782.

12. a. Use the sample mean, $\bar{X} = 29$ as the point estimate of μ.
     b. The 90% confidence interval would be
     $$\mu = 29 \pm (1.711)(2)$$
     The interval extends from 32.422 to 25.578.

13. a. With $s = 6$ and $s_{\bar{x}} = 1$, the data have a t statistic of t
     = 8.00. Reject H_o and conclude that the course has a
     significant effect.
     b. Use the sample mean, $\bar{D} = 8$ points, as the point estimate
     of μ_D.
     c. The 90% confidence interval would be
     $$\mu_D = 8 \pm (1.684)(1)$$
     which give an interval from 6.316 to 9.684.

14. a. For the experimental group, $\bar{X} = 27.0$ with $s = 2.40$. For
     the control group, $\bar{X} = 24.06$ with $s = 1.44$. The t statistic
     is $t = 3.32$. Reject H_o.
     b. The sample mean difference, 2.94 miles per gallon, is
     the best point estimate.
     c. The 90% confidence interval would be
     $$\mu_1 - \mu_2 = 2.94 \pm (1.734)(0.88)$$
     which gives an interval estimate between 4.47 and 1.41.

CHAPTER 13

INTRODUCTION TO ANALYSIS OF VARIANCE

Chapter 13 presents the general logic and basic formulas for the hypothesis testing procedure known as analysis of variance (ANOVA). The purpose of ANOVA is much the same as the t tests presented in the preceding three chapters: the goal is to determine whether the mean differences that are obtained for sample data are sufficiently large to justify a conclusion that there are mean differences between the populations from which the samples were obtained. The difference between ANOVA and the t tests is that ANOVA can be used in situations where there are <u>two or more</u> means being compared, whereas the t tests are limited to situations where only two means are involved.

Analysis of variance is necessary to protect researchers from excessive risk of a Type I error in situations where a study is comparing more than two population means. These situations would require a series of several t tests to evaluate all of the mean differences. (Remember, a t test can compare only 2 means at a time.) Although each t test can be done with a specific α-level (risk of Type I error), the α-levels accumulate over a series of tests so that the final, "experimentwise," α-level can be quite large. ANOVA allows researcher to evaluate all of the mean differences in a single hypothesis test using a single α-level and, thereby, keeps the risk of a Type I error under control no matter how many different means are being compared.

Although ANOVA can be used in a variety of different research situations, this chapter presents only independent-measures designs involving only one independent variable.

HYPOTHESIS TESTS WITH ANALYSIS OF VARIANCE (ANOVA)

The test statistic for ANOVA is an F-ratio, which is a ratio of two sample variances. In the context of ANOVA, the sample variances are called <u>mean squares</u>, or MS values. The top of the F-ratio $MS_{between}$ measures the size of mean differences between samples. The bottom of the ratio MS_{within} measures the magnitude of differences that would be expected by chance or sampling error.

Thus, the F-ratio has the same basic structure as the independent-measures t statistic presented in Chapter 10.

$$F = \frac{\text{obtained mean differences}}{\text{differences expected by chance (error)}} = \frac{MS_{between}}{MS_{within}}$$

A large value for the F-ratio indicates that the obtained sample mean differences are greater than would be expected by chance.

Each of the sample variances, MS values, in the F-ratio is computed using the basic formula for sample variance:

$$\text{sample variance} = MS = \frac{SS}{df}$$

To obtain the SS and df values, you must go through an analysis that separates the total variability for the entire set of data into two basic components: between-treatment variability (which will become the numerator of the F-ratio), and within-treatment variability (which will be the denominator). The two components of the F-ratio can be described as follows:

BETWEEN TREATMENTS VARIABILITY. $MS_{between}$ measures the size of the differences between the sample means. For example, suppose that three treatments, each with a sample of n = 5 subjects, have means of $\bar{X}_1 = 1$, $\bar{X}_2 = 2$, and $\bar{X}_3 = 3$. Notice that the three means are different; that is, they are variable. By computing the variance for the three means we can measure the size of the differences. Although it is possible to compute a variance for the set of sample means, it usually is easier to use the total, T, for each sample instead of the mean, and compute variance for the set of T values. Logically, the differences (or variance) between means can be caused by three sources:

1. Treatment Effects: If the treatments have different effects, this could cause the scores in one treatment to be higher (or lower) than the scores in another treatment.

2. Individual Differences: The individual subjects in one treatment are different from the subjects in another treatment. These individual differences could cause the scores to be different from one treatment to another.

3. Experimental Error: There is always a possibility that the differences observed in an experiment are due to error.

WITHIN TREATMENTS VARIABILITY. MS_{within} measures the size of the differences between scores within each of the samples. MS_{within} is calculated by finding the variance, s^2 for each sample, and then pooling the sample variances exactly as we did to find pooled variance for the independent-measures t statistic.

$$MS_{within} = \frac{SS_{within}}{df_{within}} = \frac{\Sigma SS}{\Sigma df} = \frac{SS_1 + SS_2 + SS_3 + \ldots}{df_1 + df_2 + df_3 + \ldots}$$

which is the same structure as

$$\text{pooled variance} = \frac{SS_1 + SS_2}{df_1 + df_2}$$

Because all the individuals in a sample receive exactly the same treatment, any differences (or variance) within a sample can be caused by only two sources:

1. Individual Differences: The scores come from different subjects which could cause them to be different.

2. Experimental Error: Again, there is always a possibility that the observed differences are simply due to error.

Considering these sources of variability, the structure of the F-ratio becomes,

$$F = \frac{\text{treatment effect + individual differences + error}}{\text{individual differences + error}}$$

When the null hypothesis is true and there are no differences between treatments, the F-ratio is balanced. That is, when the "treatment effect" is zero, the top and bottom of the F-ratio are measuring the same variance. In this case, you should expect an F-ratio near 1.00. When the sample data produce an F-ratio near 1.00, we will conclude that there is no significant treatment effect.

On the other hand, a large treatment effect will produce a large value for the F-ratio. Thus, when the sample data produce a large F-ratio we will reject the null hypothesis and conclude that there are significant differences between treatments.

To determine whether an F-ratio is large enough to be significant, you must select an α-level, find the df values for the numerator and denominator of the F-ratio, and consult the F-distribution table to find the critical value.

ANOVA AND POST TESTS

The null hypothesis for ANOVA states that for the general population there are no mean differences among the treatments being compared; H_O: $\mu_1 = \mu_2 = \mu_3 = \ldots$

When the null hypothesis is rejected, the conclusion is that there are significant mean differences. However, the ANOVA simply establishes that differences exist, it does not indicate exactly which treatments are different. With more than two treatments, this creates a problem. Specifically, you must follow the ANOVA with additional tests, called <u>post tests</u>, to determine exactly which treatments are different and which are not. The Scheffe test and Tukey's HSD test are examples of post tests. These tests are done after an ANOVA where H_O is rejected with more than two treatment conditions. The tests compare the treatments, two at a time, to test for mean differences.

ANOVA AND THE INDEPENDENT-MEASURES t TEST

When a research study compares only two treatments using an independent-measures design, the data may be analyzed using either an analysis of variance or an independent-measures t test. The two procedures evaluate exactly the same hypotheses and always will reach exactly the same conclusion. In addition, the t statistic obtained from the data and the F-ratio obtained from the data are directly related by $F = t^2$. The critical values for t and F are also related by $F = t^2$. Finally, the df value for the t statistic (associated with the pooled variance) will be equal to the df value for MS_{within} (the denominator of the F-ratio which also is measuring pooled variance).

LEARNING OBJECTIVES

---

1.   You should be familiar with the purpose, terminology, and special notation of analysis of variance.

2. You should be able to perform an analysis of variance for the data from a single-factor, independent-measures experiment.

3. You should recognize when post hoc tests are necessary and you should be able to complete an analysis of variance using Tukey's HSD or the Scheffe' post hoc test.

4. You should be able to report the results of an analysis of variance using either a summary table or an F-ratio (including df values). Also, you should be able to understand and interpret these reports when they appear in scientific literature.

NEW TERMS AND CONCEPTS

The following terms were introduced in this chapter. Define or describe each term and, where appropriate, describe how each term is related to other terms in the list.

factor
levels of a factor
F-ratio
error term
MS (Mean Square)
post hoc test
between treatments SS, df, and MS
within treatments SS, df, and MS
total SS and df

$$SS_{total} = \Sigma X^2 - \frac{G^2}{N} \qquad\qquad df_{total} = N - 1$$

$$SS_{between} = \Sigma \frac{T^2}{n} - \frac{G^2}{N} \qquad\qquad df_{between} = k - 1$$

$$SS_{within} = \Sigma SS_{each\ treatment} \qquad\qquad df_{within} = N - k$$

$$MS = \frac{SS}{df} \qquad\qquad F = \frac{MS_{between}}{MS_{within}}$$

STEP BY STEP

Analysis of Variance: Analysis of variance is a hypothesis testing technique that is used to determine whether there are differences among the means of two or more populations. In this chapter we examined ANOVA for an independent-measures experiment, which means that the data consist of a separate sample for each treatment condition (or each population). Before you begin the actual analysis, you should complete all the preliminary calculations with the data, including T and SS for each sample and G and ΣX^2 for the entire set of scores. The following example will be used to demonstrate ANOVA.

A researcher has obtained three different samples representing three populations. The data are presented below.

Sample 1	Sample 2	Sample 3	
0	6	6	
4	8	5	$G = 60$
0	5	9	
1	4	4	$\Sigma X^2 = 356$
0	2	6	

T = 5	T = 25	T = 30
SS = 12	SS = 20	SS = 14

Step 1: State the hypotheses and select an alpha level. The null hypothesis states that there are no mean differences among the three populations.

$$H_o: \mu_1 = \mu_2 = \mu_3$$

Remember, we generally do not try to list specific alternatives, but rather state a generic alternative hypothesis.

H_1: At least one population mean is different from the others

For this test we will use $\alpha = .05$.

Step 2: Locate the critical region. With k = 3 samples, the numerator of the F-ratio will have $df_{between}$ = k - 1 = 2. There are n = 5 scores in each sample. Within each sample there are n - 1 = 4 degrees of freedom, and summing across all three samples gives

$$df_{within} = 4 + 4 + 4 = 12$$

for the denominator of the F-ratio. Thus, the F-ratio for this analysis will have df = 2,12.

Sketch the entire distribution of F-ratios with df = 2,12 and locate the extreme 5% of the distribution. The critical F value is 3.88.

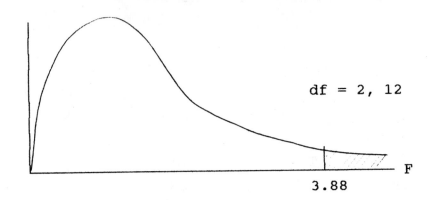

df = 2, 12

3.88

Step 3: Compute the test statistic. It is best to work through the calculations in a systematic way. Compute all three parts of the analysis (total, between, and within) and check that the two components add to the total.

$$SS_{total} = \Sigma X^2 - \frac{G^2}{N} = 356 - \frac{(60)^2}{15}$$

$$= 356 - 240$$

$$= 116$$

$$SS_{bet} = \Sigma \frac{T^2}{n} - \frac{G^2}{N} = \frac{(5)^2}{5} + \frac{(25)^2}{5} + \frac{(30)^2}{5} - \frac{(60)^2}{15}$$

$$= 5 + 125 + 180 - 240$$

$$= 70$$

$$SS_{within} = \Sigma SS = 12 + 20 + 14 = 46$$

(Check that 116 = 70 + 46)

We have already found $df_{between}$ and df_{within}. To complete the analysis of df, compute

$$df_{total} = N - 1 = 15 - 1 = 14$$

(Check that $14 = 12 + 2$)

Next, compute the two variances (Mean Squares) that will form the F-ratio.

$$MS_{between} = \frac{SS_{between}}{df_{between}} = \frac{70}{2} = 35$$

$$MS_{within} = \frac{SS_{within}}{df_{within}} = \frac{46}{12} = 3.83$$

Finally, the F-ratio for these data is,

$$F = \frac{MS_{between}}{MS_{within}} = \frac{35}{3.83} = 9.14$$

Step 4: Make decision. The F-ratio for these data is in the critical region. The numerator is more than 9 times larger than the denominator which indicates a significant treatment effect. Reject H_o and conclude that there are differences among the means of the three populations.

1.   It may help you to understand analysis of variance if you
      remember that measuring variance is conceptually the same as
      measuring differences. The goal of the analysis is to
      determine whether the mean differences in the data are
      larger than would be expected by chance.

2.   The formulas for SS between treatments and SS within
      treatments, and their role in the F-ratio may be easier
      to remember if you look at the similarities between the
      independent measures t formula and the F-ratio formula.
      a.   The numerator of the t statistic measures the
            difference between the two sample means, $(\bar{X}_1 - \bar{X}_2)$. The
            numerator of the F-ratio also looks at differences
            between treatments by computing the variability for the
            treatment totals.
      b.   The standard error in the denominator of the t
            statistic is computed by first pooling the two sample
            variances. This calculation uses the SS values from
            each of the two separate samples. The denominator of
            the F-ratio also uses the SS values from each of the
            separate samples to compute SS within treatments. In
            fact, when there are only two treatment conditions, the
            pooled variance from the t statistic is equivalent to
            the MS within treatments from the F-ratio.

1. It is impossible to obtain a negative value for an F- ratio. (True or False)

2. If the null hypothesis is true, the F-ratio for ANOVA is expected (on average) to have a value of _____.

3. An F-ratio of zero (F = 0) indicates that all of the separate samples have exactly the same mean. (True or False)

4. In an analysis of variance, the larger the differences between the sample means, the bigger the value for the F-ratio. (Assume that all other factors are held constant.) (True or False)

5. A researcher reports an F-ratio with df = 2, 30 for an independent measures experiment.
    a. How many treatment conditions were compared in the experiment?
    b. How many subjects participated in the experiment?

6. The critical region for an analysis of variance is located entirely in one tail of the distribution. (True or False)

7. Post tests are used after an analysis of variance to determine whether or not a Type I error was made during the ANOVA. (True or False)

8. Post tests are done after an analysis of variance when the statistical decision is "Fail to Reject H_o." (True or False)

9. Post tests are <u>not</u> necessary if there are only two treatments in the original ANOVA. (True or False)

10. A researcher conducts an experiment comparing four treatment conditions with a separate sample of $n = 5$ in each treatment. An analysis of variance is used to evaluate the data, and the results of the ANOVA are presented in the table below. Complete all missing values in the table.

Source	SS	df	MS	
Between Treatments	12	__	__	$F = 2.00$
Within Treatments	__	__	__	
Total	__	__		

11. The following data summarize the results of two experiments. Each experiment compares three treatment conditions, and each experiment uses separate samples of $n = 10$ for each treatment.

	Experiment 1 Treatment				Experiment 2 Treatment		
	1	2	3		1	2	3
	$\bar{X} = 1$	$\bar{X} = 3$	$\bar{X} = 5$		$\bar{X} = 1$	$\bar{X} = 10$	$\bar{X} = 20$
	$s = 15$	$s = 12$	$s = 18$		$s = 3$	$s = 5$	$s = 4$

Just looking at the data - without doing any calculations - answer each of the following questions.

     a.   Which experiment will produce the larger $MS_{between}$?

     b.   Which experiment will produce the larger MS_{within}?

     c.   Which experiment will produce the larger F-ratio?

12. Use an analysis of variance with α = .05 to determine whether the following data provide evidence of any significant differences among the three treatments.

Treatments

I	II	III	
0	4	1	G = 30
2	6	0	
2	1	3	ΣX^2 = 114
0	5	1	
1	4	0	
T = 5	T = 20	T = 5	
SS = 4	SS = 14	SS = 6	

13. The following data are from two separate samples.

   a. Use an analysis of variance with α = .05 to determine whether these data provide evidence for a significant difference between the two population means.

   b. If you had used a t test instead of ANOVA, what value would you have obtained for the t statistic?

Sample 1	Sample 2
n = 10	n = 10
$\bar{X}$ = 3	$\bar{X}$ = 5
SS = 200	SS = 160

===

ANSWERS TO SELF-TEST

===

1. True. An F-ratio is a ratio of two variances which are squared values (always positive).

2. When the null hypothesis is true, the top and bottom of the F-ratio are measuring the same variance. In this case, the expected value for F is 1.00.

3. True. $F = 0$ indicates that there is zero variability (no difference) among the treatment means.

4. True. The numerator of the F-ratio measures the size of the mean differences between treatments. The larger the mean differences, the larger the F-ratio.

5.   a. $k = 3$ treatments $(df_{between} = k - 1 = 2)$
       b. $N = 33$ subjects $(df_{within} = N - k = 30)$

6. True. Extremely large values of F indicate that the differences between treatments (numerator) are significantly larger than chance (measured by MS_{within} in the denominator.)

7. False. Post tests are done to determine exactly which treatment conditions are significantly different.

8. False. Post tests are necessary only when you reject H_o.

9. True. With only two treatments there is no question as to which treatments are significantly different.

10.

Source	SS	df	MS	
Between Treatments	12	3	4	$F = 2.00$
Within Treatments	32	16	2	
Total	44	19		

11.   a.   Experiment 2 has larger mean differences and will produce a larger $MS_{between}$.
       b.   Experiment 1 has larger sample standard deviations (more variance within samples) and will produce a larger MS_{within}.
       c.   Experiment 2 has larger differences between treatments and smaller variability within treatments. This combination will produce a larger F-ratio.

12. The ANOVA is summarized as follows:

Source	SS	df	MS	
Between Treatments	30	2	15	F = 7.50
Within Treatments	24	12	2	
Total	54	14		

With df = 2, 12 the critical value is F = 3.88. Reject H_o and conclude that there are significant differences among the three treatments.

13. a. With df = 1,18 the critical value for F is 4.41. For these data,

Source	SS	df	MS	
Between Treatments	20	1	20	F = 1.00
Within Treatments	360	18	20	
Total	380	19		

Fail to reject H_o.

b. The t test would produce a t statistic of
$t = \sqrt{F} = 1.00$.

CHAPTER 14

REPEATED-MEASURES
ANALYSIS OF VARIANCE

CHAPTER SUMMARY

Chapter 14 extends analysis of variance to research situations using repeated-measures or related-samples research designs. Much of the logic and many of the formulas for repeated-measures ANOVA are identical to the independent-measures analysis introduced in Chapter 13. However, the repeated-measures ANOVA includes a second stage of analysis in which variability due to individual differences is subtracted out of the error term. The repeated-measures design eliminates individual differences from the between-treatments variability because the same subjects are used in every treatment condition. To balance the F-ratio, however, the calculations require that individual differences also be eliminated from the denominator of the F-ratio. The result is a test statistic similar to the independent-measures F-ratio but with all individual differences removed.

Previously, in Chapter 13, we examined the independent-measures analysis of variance (ANOVA). It is used in situations when the number of treatments or levels is two or more ($k \geq 2$). Also, a separate independent sample is used for each level. For example, if there are three treatment conditions, then three separate samples are used, one for each treatment. The analysis compares the mean square (MS) between treatments to mean square within treatments in the form of a ratio

$$F = \frac{MS_{\text{between treatments}}}{MS_{\text{within treatments}}}$$

Now, in Chapter 14, we have a repeated-measures study with $k \geq 2$ levels, however one sample of subjects serves for every (k) level of the treatment. So, if there are $k = 3$ levels for a treatment, the same sample of individuals would be tested, first for one treatment level, then for the next level, and finally for the last. What makes the repeated-measures study interesting is how it treats variability from individual differences. Recall that the independent-measures F ratio (chapter 13) has the following structure:

$$F = \frac{MS_{\text{between treatments}}}{MS_{\text{within}}}$$

$$= \frac{\text{treatment effect} + \text{individual differences} + \text{error}}{\text{individual differences} + \text{error}}$$

In this formula, when the treatment effect is zero (H_o true), the expected F ratio is one.

In the repeated-measures study, individual differences do not play a role in the between-treatments variability because the same sample is tested for every treatment. This means that variability due to individual differences is not a component of the numerator of the F ratio. Therefore, it must be removed from the denominator of the F ratio so that the expected value will remain one when the treatment effect is zero. That is, we want the structural formula to be

$$F = \frac{\text{treatment effect} + \text{error}}{\text{error}}$$

This is accomplished by a two-stage analysis. In the first stage, total variability (SS_{total}) is partitioned into the between- treatments SS and within-treatments SS. (Note, this is the same process we used for the independent-measures ANOVA.) The components for between-treatments variability are the treatment effect (if any) and error. Individual differences do not appear here because the same sample of subjects serves in every treatment. On the other hand, individual differences do play a role in SS_{within} because the sample contains different (n) subjects.

In the second stage of the analysis, we determine individual differences by computing the variability between subjects, or $SS_{between\ subjects}$. This value is subtracted from SS_{within} leaving a remainder, variability due to experimental error, SS_{error}. This two stage process is outlined in Figure 14.2 of your text.

A similar two-stage analysis is done with degrees of freedom (Figure 14.3 of your text), allowing the computation of the mean square values. For the repeated-measures study, the mean squares and F are

$$MS_{treatments} = \frac{SS_{between\ treatments}}{df_{between\ treatments}}$$

$$MS_{error} = \frac{SS_{error}}{df_{error}} \qquad F = \frac{MS_{between\ treatments}}{MS_{error}}$$

One of the main advantages of the repeated-measures design is that the role of individual differences can be eliminated from the study. This advantage can be a very important in situations where large individual differences would otherwise obscure the treatment effect in an independent-measures study.

LEARNING OBJECTIVES

1.   Be able to explain the logic of the repeated-measures ANOVA.

2.   Understand how variability is partitioned and what sources of variability contribute to each component.

3.   Know the difference between the analysis for repeated-versus independent-measures designs.

4.   Be able to perform the computations for a complete analysis.

NEW TERMS AND CONCEPTS

The following terms were introduced in this chapter. Define or describe each term and, where appropriate, describe how each term is related to other terms in the list.

    between-treatments variability
    within-treatments variability
    between-subjects variability
    error variability
    treatment effect
    individual differences
    experimental error
    F-ratio

NEW FORMULAS

In addition to the total SS, between-treatments SS, within-treatments SS, and the corresponding df and MS values that were presented in Chapter 13, several new formulas are introduced in Chapter 14:

$$SS_{\text{between subjects}} = \Sigma\frac{P^2}{k} - \frac{G^2}{N}$$

$$df_{\text{between subjects}} = n - 1$$

$$SS_{\text{error}} = SS_{\text{within}} - SS_{\text{between subjects}}$$

$$df_{\text{error}} = df_{\text{within}} - df_{\text{between subjects}}$$
$$= (N - k) - (n - 1)$$

STEP BY STEP

The repeated-measures ANOVA is used to determine whether there are any differences among the means of two or more different treatments using the data from a single sample that has been measured in each treatment condition. The calculations and notation for the repeated-measures ANOVA are very similar to the independent-measures design. In fact, the first stage of the repeated-measures analysis is identical to the independent ANOVA. However, the repeated analysis continues through a second stage where the individual differences are removed from the denominator of the F-ratio. The following example will be used to demonstrate the repeated-measures ANOVA.

A researcher is comparing four different treatment conditions using a repeated-measures experiment with a sample of n = 6 subjects. The data from this experiment are as follows:

Treatment

Subject	1	2	3	4	P
#1	0	2	6	0	8
#2	4	0	7	1	12
#3	5	4	11	0	20
#4	8	7	13	4	32
#5	7	2	9	2	20
#6	6	3	14	5	28
T	30	18	60	12	
SS	40	28	52	22	

$$G = 120 \qquad \Sigma X^2 = 970$$

Step 1: State the hypotheses and select an alpha level. The null hypothesis states that there are no differences among the means for the four treatment conditions.

$$H_0: \quad \mu_1 = \mu_2 = \mu_3 = \mu_4$$

The general alternative hypothesis is,

H_1: At least one of the treatment means is different from the others.

We will use $\alpha = .05$.

Step 2: Locate the critical region. The first problem is to determine the df values for the F-ratio. We will conduct a complete analysis of df to determine $df_{between}$ and df_{error}. For these data,

$$df_{total} = N - 1 = 24 - 1 = 23$$
$$df_{between} = k - 1 = 4 - 1 = 3$$
$$df_{within} = N - k = 24 - 4 = 20$$

This completes the first stage of the analysis. (Check to be sure that the total equals the sum of the two components.) For the second stage,

$$df_{subjects} = n - 1 = 6 - 1 = 5$$

$$df_{error} = df_{within} - df_{subjects}$$
$$= 20 - 5$$
$$= 15$$

The F-ratio will have df = 3, 15. Sketch the entire distribution of F-ratios with df = 3,15 and locate the extreme 5% of the distribution. The critical F value is 3.29.

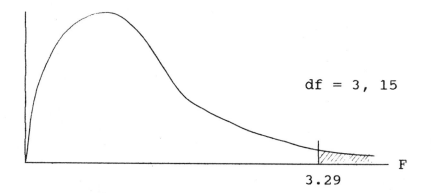

df = 3, 15

3.29

Step 3: Compute the test statistic. We have completed the analysis for df, so we will continue with the analysis of SS. As before, we will complete the analysis in two stages.

$$SS_{total} = \Sigma X^2 - \frac{G^2}{N}$$

$$= 970 - \frac{120^2}{24} = 970 - 600 = 370$$

$$SS_{between} = \Sigma \frac{T^2}{n} - \frac{G^2}{N}$$

$$= \frac{30^2}{6} + \frac{18^2}{6} + \frac{60^2}{6} + \frac{12^2}{6} - \frac{120^2}{24}$$

$$= 150 + 54 + 600 + 24 - 600$$

$$= 228$$

$$SS_{within} = \Sigma SS = 40 + 28 + 52 + 22 = 142$$

This completes the first stage. (Check to be sure that the two components add to the total.) Continuing with the second stage,

$$SS_{subjects} = \Sigma \frac{P^2}{k} - \frac{G^2}{N}$$

$$= \frac{8^2}{4} + \frac{12^2}{4} + \frac{20^2}{4} + \frac{32^2}{4} + \frac{20^2}{4} + \frac{28^2}{4} - \frac{120^2}{24}$$

$$= 16 + 36 + 100 + 256 + 100 + 196 - 600$$

$$= 704 - 600 = 104$$

$$SS_{error} = SS_{within} - SS_{subjects}$$

$$= 142 - 104$$

$$= 38$$

Next, compute the two Mean Squares that will form the F-ratio.

$$MS_{between} = \frac{SS_{between}}{df_{between}} = 228/3 = 76$$

$$MS_{error} = \frac{SS_{error}}{df_{error}} = 38/15 = 2.53$$

Finally, the F-ratio for these data is,

$$F = \frac{MS_{between}}{MS_{error}} = 76/2.53 = 30.04$$

Step 4: Make decision. The F-ratio for these data is in the critical region. This is a very unlikely value to be obtained if H_o is true. Therefore, we reject H_o and conclude that there are significant differences among the four treatment means.

===========

HINTS AND CAUTIONS
===========

1. In the repeated-measures ANOVA, it is important that you remember to use the correct error term (denominator) for the F-ratio, namely MS_{error}.

2. A very common mistake when locating the critical region for a repeated-measures F-ratio is to use within treatments df. Remember, the correct df value for the error term is the error df.

3. One important fact that may help you to remember the structure and the value of a repeated-measures ANOVA is that the repeated measures design eliminates individual differences. The individual differences do not exist in the numerator of the F-ratio because the same individuals are used in all of the treatment conditions. In the denominator of the F-ratio there are no individual differences because they are subtracted out in the second stage of the analysis.

4. In the typical display of data for a repeated-measures experiment the scores for each subject are listed in rows

and the scores for each treatment are listed in columns (see the Step-by-Step example). When you are computing $SS_{between}$ you are measuring the differences between columns of data. When you compute $SS_{subjects}$ you are measuring the differences between rows of data. This observation should help you recognize the similarity between the formulas for these two SS values.

$$SS_{between} = \Sigma\frac{T^2}{n} - \frac{G^2}{N}$$

$$SS_{subjects} = \Sigma\frac{P^2}{k} - \frac{G^2}{N}$$

SELF-TEST AND REVIEW

1. The first stage of the repeated-measures ANOVA is the same as the independent-measures ANOVA. (True or False)

2. The P totals are necessary to compute $SS_{between\ treatments}$. (True or False)

3. In the second stage of ANOVA for repeated measures, you compute the value for SS_{error} and subtract it from SS_{within} to find the correct error term for the F ratio. (True or False)

4. The final F-ratio in the repeated-measures analysis is structured so that it has an expected value of 1.00 when the null hypothesis is true.
    a. What sources of variability contribute to the numerator of the F-ratio ($MS_{between\ treatments}$)?
    b. Explain why "individual differences" is not listed as a source of variability in the numerator.

c. What sources of variability contribute to the denominator of the F-ratio (MS_{error})?

d. Explain why "individual differences" is not listed as a source of variability in the denominator.

5. If individual differences are large for a particular dependent variable, a repeated-measures study is more likely to detect a treatment effect than an independent-measures study. (True or False)

6. An industrial researcher tests 3 different keyboard designs for a new computer to determine which one produces optimal performance. Four computer operators are given text material and are told to type the material as fast as they can. They spend 3 minutes on each keyboard with a 5 minute rest between each trial. The number of errors committed are recorded. Do the following data indicate a significant difference among the 3 keyboard types? Test at the .05 level of significance.

Operator	1	2	3	P	
#1	6	2	4	12	
#2	8	6	7	21	
#3	3	6	9	18	$\Sigma X^2 = 360$
#4	3	2	4	9	
T	20	16	24		G = 60
SS	18	16	18		

7. A sample of n = 7 individuals is selected to participate in a learning study. Each individual is tested at five different stages during learning (after 1 hour, 2 hours, 3 hours, etc.). The data from this experiment were examined using a repeated-measures ANOVA to determine whether there was any

evidence of a practice effect. The results are presented in the following summary table. Complete all the missing values in the table. Hint: Begin with the df column.

Source	SS	df	MS	
Between Treatments	____	____	10	F = ____
Within Treatments	____	____		
Between Subjects	52	____		
Error	____	____	____	
Total	140	____		

8.   A toy manufacturer is testing 3 versions of a toy that is under development. Among other things, the manufacturer would like to see which version of the toy attracts the most attention. A psychologist allows a child to play with all 3 toys and records the amount of time (in minutes) spent playing with each. A sample of n = 5 children is used. Use the following data to determine whether there is a significant preference among the three toys. Use the .05 level of significance.

Toy

Child	1	2	3
A	0	2	4
B	2	2	8
C	3	1	5
D	0	3	6
E	0	2	7

1.   True. Total SS is partitioned into between-treatments SS and within-treatments SS.

2.   False. The P values are used to obtain between-subjects SS, the measure of variability due to individual differences.

3.   False. Between-subjects SS is computed first. It is subtracted from within-treatment SS to yield error SS. SS_{error} is used to compute the error term for the F ratio, MS_{error}.

4.   a. The numerator of the F-ratio contains variability from treatment effects and experimental error.
      b. There are no individual differences in the variability between treatments because the same individuals are used in every treatment.
      c. The denominator of the F-ratio contains variability from experimental error.
      d. There are no individual differences in the denominator because they are subtracted out in the second stage of the analysis.

5.   True. For the independent-measures design, the numerator ($MS_{between\ treatments}$) and the denominator (MS_{within}) contain variability due to individual differences. If this variability is large it will obscure a treatment effect. This is not a problem with the repeated-measures design because individual differences have been removed from the analysis.

6.   The null hypothesis states that there are no differences among the three keyboard types. With df = 2,6 the critical value is F = 5.14.

Source	SS	df	MS	
Between Treatments	8	2	4	F = 1.09
Within Treatments	52	9		
Between Subjects	30	3		
Error	22	6	3.67	
Total	60	11		

Fail to reject H_o. There are no significant differences among the three keyboard types.

7.

Source	SS	df	MS	
Between Treatments	40	4	10	F = 5.00
Within Treatments	100	30		
Between Subjects	52	6		
Error	48	24	2	
Total	140	34		

8. The null hypothesis states that there are no differences among the 3 toys. With df = 2,8, the critical boundary is F = 4.46.

Source	SS	df	MS	
Between Treatments	70	2	35	F = 20
Within Treatments	20	12		
Between Subjects	6	4		
Error	14	8	1.75	
Total	90	14		

Reject the null hypothesis and conclude that there are significant differences among the three toys.

CHAPTER SUMMARY

Chapter 15 extends analysis of variance to research designs that involve two independent variables. In the context of ANOVA, an independent variable is called a factor, and research studies with two factors are called <u>factorial designs</u> or simply <u>two-factor designs</u>. The two factors are identified as A and B, and the structure of a two-factor design can be represented as a matrix with the levels of factor A determining the rows and the levels of factor B determining the columns. For example, a researcher studying the effects of heat and humidity on performance could use the following experimental design:

FACTOR B
HEAT
TEMPERATURE IN °F

		80°	90°	100°
	LOW	sample 1	sample 2	sample 3
FACTOR A HUMIDITY	HIGH	sample 4	sample 5	sample 6

Notice that the study involves two levels of humidity and three levels of heat, creating a two-by-three matrix with a total of 6 different treatment conditions. Each treatment condition is represented by a cell in the matrix. For an independent-measures experiment, a separate sample would be used for each of the six conditions.

The goal for the two-factor ANOVA is to determine whether the mean differences that are observed for the sample data are sufficiently large to conclude that they are <u>significant</u> differences and not simply the result of sampling error. For the example we are considering, the goal is to determine whether different levels of heat and humidity produce significant differences in performance. To evaluate the sample mean differences, a two-factor ANOVA conducts three separate and independent hypothesis tests. The three tests evaluate:

1. <u>The Main Effect for Factor A</u>: The mean differences between the levels of factor A are obtained by computing the overall mean for each row in the matrix. In this example, the main effect of factor A would compare the overall mean performance with high humidity versus the overall mean performance with low humidity.

2. <u>The Main Effect for Factor B</u>: The mean differences between the levels of factor B are obtained by computing the overall mean for each column in the matrix. In this example, the ANOVA would compare the overall mean performance at 80° versus 90° versus 100°.

3. <u>The A x B Interaction</u>: Often two factors will "interact" so that specific combinations of the two factors produce results (mean differences) that are not explained by the overall effects of either factor. For example, changes

in humidity (factor A) may have a relatively small overall effect on performance when the temperature is low. However, when the temperature is high (100°), the effects of humidity may be exaggerated. In this case, unique combinations of heat and humidity produce results that are not explained by the overall main effects. These "extra" mean differences are the interaction.

The primary advantage of combining two factors (independent variables) in a single research study is that it allows you to examine how the two factors interact with each other. That is, the results will not only show the overall main effects of each factor, but also how unique combinations of the two variables may produce unique results. The interaction can be defined as "extra" mean differences, beyond the main effects of the two factors. An alternative definition is that an interaction exists when the effects of one factor depend on the levels of the second factor.

THE TWO-FACTOR ANALYSIS

Each of the three hypothesis tests in a two-factor ANOVA will have its own F-ratio and each F-ratio has the same basic structure

$$F = \frac{\text{variance (differences) between means}}{\text{variance (differences) from error}} = \frac{MS_{between}}{MS_{within}}$$

Each MS value equals SS/df, and the individual SS and df values are computed in a two-state analysis. The first stage of the analysis is identical to the single-factor ANOVA (Chapter 13) and separates the total variability (SS and df) into two basic components: Between Treatments and Within Treatments. The between-treatments variability measures the magnitude of the mean differences between treatment conditions (the individual cells in the data matrix) and is computed using the basic formulas for $SS_{between}$ and $df_{between}$.

$$SS_{between} = \Sigma \frac{T^2}{n} - \frac{G^2}{N}$$

where the T values (totals) are the cell totals and n is the number of scores in each cell

$$df_{between} = \text{the number of cells (totals) minus one}$$

The within-treatments variability measures the magnitude of the differences within each treatment condition (cell) and provides a measure of error variance; that is, unexplained, unpredicted differences due to error.

$$MS_{within} = \frac{SS_{within}}{df_{within}} = \frac{\Sigma SS}{\Sigma df} = \frac{SS_1 + SS_2 + SS_3 + \ldots}{df_1 + df_2 + df_3 + \ldots}$$

All three F-ratios use same denominator, MS_{within}, as the error term.

The second stage of the analysis separates the between-treatments variability into the three components that will form the numerators for the three F-ratios: Variance due to factor A, variance due to factor B, and variance due to the interaction. Each of the three variances (MS) measures the differences for a specific set of sample means. The main effect for factor A, for example, will measure the mean differences between rows of the data matrix. The actual formulas for each SS and df are based on the sample totals (rather than the means) and all have the same structure:

$$SS_{between} = \Sigma \frac{T^2}{n} - \frac{G^2}{N}$$

$$= \Sigma \frac{(Total)^2}{number} - \frac{G^2}{N}$$

where the "number" is the number of scores that are summed to obtain each Total

$$df_{between} = \text{the number of means (or totals) minus one}$$

For factor A, the Totals are the row totals and df equals the number of rows minus 1.

For factor B, the Totals are the column totals and df equals the number of columns minus 1.

The interaction measures the "extra" mean differences that exist after the main effects for factor A and factor B have been considered. The SS and df values for the interaction are found by subtraction.

$$SS_{A \times B} = SS_{bet\ cells} - SS_A - SS_B$$

$$df_{A \times B} = df_{bet\ cells} - df_A - df_B = (df_A)(df_B)$$

LEARNING OBJECTIVES

1. Be able to conduct a two-factor ANOVA to evaluate the data from an independent-measures experiment that uses two independent variables.

2. Understand the definition of an interaction between two factors, and be able to recognize an interaction from a description or a graph of experimental results.

3. Be familiar with the use of a two-factor design as a means of controlling variability within treatments.

NEW TERMS AND CONCEPTS

The following terms were introduced in this chapter. Define or describe each term and, where appropriate, describe how each term is related to other terms in the list.

two-factor experiment
matrix and cells
main effect
interaction
factor A
factor B
a   (number of levels of factor A)
b   (number of levels of factor B)

NEW FORMULAS

$$SS_{total} = \Sigma X^2 - \frac{G^2}{N} \qquad df_{total} = N - 1$$

$$SS_{bet.\ cells} = \Sigma \frac{AB^2}{n} - \frac{G^2}{N} \qquad df_{bet.\ cells} = ab - 1$$

$$SS_{within} = \Sigma SS_{each\ cell} \qquad df_{within} = N - ab$$

$$SS_{factor\ A} = \Sigma\frac{A^2}{bn} - \frac{G^2}{N} \qquad df_{factor\ A} = a - 1$$

$$SS_{factor\ B} = \Sigma\frac{B^2}{an} - \frac{G^2}{N} \qquad df_{factor\ B} = b - 1$$

$$SS_{AxB} = SS_{bet\ cells} - SS_A - SS_B$$

$$df_{AxB} = df_A df_B = (a - 1)(b - 1)$$

STEP BY STEP

Two-Factor ANOVA. The two-factor analysis of variance is used for experimental data with two independent variables. The two factors are generally identified as A and B, and the data are presented in a matrix with the levels of factor A determining the rows and the levels of factor B determining the columns. The analysis of variance evaluates three separate hypotheses: one concerning the main effect of factor A, one concerning the main effect of factor B, and one concerning the interaction. In this chapter we considered the two-factor analysis for an independent-measures experiment which means that the data consist of a separate sample for each AB treatment combination. The following example will be used to demonstrate the two-factor ANOVA.

The following data are from a two-factor experiment with a = 2 levels of factor A and b = 3 levels of factor B. There are n = 10 subjects in each treatment condition.

Factor B

	B1	B2	B3	
A1	AB = 10 SS = 20	AB = 20 SS = 32	AB = 30 SS = 35	$A_1 = 60$
A2	AB = 10 SS = 15	AB = 10 SS = 35	AB = 10 SS = 25	$A_2 = 30$

Factor A

$B_1 = 20 \qquad B_2 = 30 \qquad B_3 = 40 \qquad G = 90$

$$\Sigma X^2 = 332$$

Step 1:   State the hypotheses and select an alpha level. Because the two-factor ANOVA evaluates three separate hypotheses, there will be three null hypotheses.

For Factor A: H_0: $\mu_{A1} = \mu_{A2}$ (no A-effect)
  H_1: $\mu_{A1} \neq \mu_{A2}$

For Factor B: H_0: $\mu_{B1} = \mu_{B2} = \mu_{B3}$ (no B-effect)
  H_1:   At least one of the B means is different from the others

For AxB: H_0:   There is no interaction between factors A and B. That is, the effect of either factor does not depend on the levels of the other factor.
  H_1:   There is an A x B interaction

We will use $\alpha = .05$ for all three tests.

Step 2: Locate the critical regions. Because there are
three separate tests, each with its own F-ratio, we will
need to determine the critical region for each test
separately. We begin by analyzing the degrees of freedom
for these data to determine df for each F. The analysis
proceeds in two stages.

$$df_{total} = N - 1 = 60 - 1 = 59$$
$$df_{bet\ cells} = ab - 1 = 6 - 1 = 5$$
$$df_{within} = N - ab = 60 - 6 = 54$$

This completes the first stage of the analysis. (Check
to be certain that the two components add to the total.)

Continuing with the second stage,

$$df_A = a - 1 = 2 - 1 = 1$$
$$df_B = b - 1 = 3 - 1 = 2$$
$$df_{AxB} = (df_A)(df_B) = 1(2) = 2$$

Again, check to be certain that the three components from
the second stage add to $df_{bet\ cells}$.

For these data, factor A will have an F-ratio with df =
1,54. Factor B and the AxB interaction both will have F-
ratios with df = 2,54. Thus, we need F distributions and
critical regions for two separate df values. Sketch the two
distributions and locate the extreme 5% in each. (Because
df = 54 is not listed, we have used 55 for the denominator
in each case.)

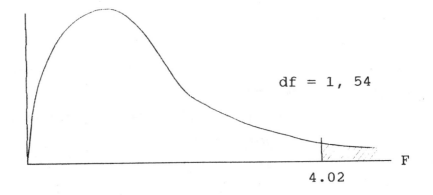

df = 1, 54

4.02

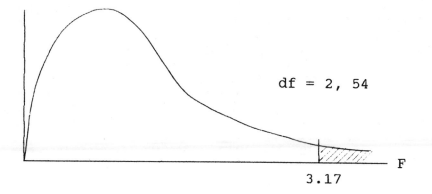

df = 2, 54

3.17

F

Step 3: Calculate the test statistic. Again, we will need three separate F-ratios. We already have analyzed the degrees of freedom for these data, so we will continue with the analysis of SS. As before, the analysis proceeds in two stages.

$$SS_{total} = \Sigma X^2 - \frac{G^2}{N}$$

$$= 332 - \frac{90^2}{60} = 332 - 135 = 197$$

$$SS_{bet.\ cells} = \Sigma \frac{AB^2}{n} - \frac{G^2}{N}$$

$$= \frac{10^2}{10} + \frac{20^2}{10} + \frac{30^2}{10} + \frac{10^2}{10} + \frac{10^2}{10} + \frac{10^2}{10} - \frac{90^2}{60}$$

$$= 10 + 40 + 90 + 10 + 10 + 10 - 135$$

$$= 35$$

$$SS_{within} = \Sigma SS = 20 + 32 + 35 + 15 + 35 + 25$$

$$= 162$$

This completes stage one. Be sure that the two components add to the total.

Chapter 15 - page 189

For the second stage,

$$SS_A = \Sigma \frac{A^2}{bn} - \frac{G^2}{N}$$

$$= \frac{60^2}{30} + \frac{30^2}{30} - \frac{90^2}{60}$$

$$= 120 + 30 - 135$$

$$= 15$$

$$SS_B = \Sigma \frac{B^2}{an} - \frac{G^2}{N}$$

$$= \frac{20^2}{20} + \frac{30^2}{20} + \frac{40^2}{20} - \frac{90^2}{60}$$

$$= 20 + 45 + 80 - 135$$

$$= 10$$

$$SS_{A \times B} = SS_{bet \ cells} - SS_A - SS_B$$

$$= 35 - 15 - 10$$

$$= 10$$

Again, check that these three components from stage two add to $SS_{bet \ cells}$.

Next, compute the MS values that will become the numerators for the three F-ratios.

$$MS_A = \frac{SS_A}{df_A} = 15/1 = 15$$

$$MS_B = \frac{SS_B}{df_B} = 10/2 = 5$$

$$MS_{A \times B} = \frac{SS_{A \times B}}{df_{A \times B}} = 10/2 = 5$$

All three F-ratios will have the same error term (denominator):

$$MS_{within} = \frac{SS_{within}}{df_{within}} = 162/54 = 3$$

Finally, the three F-ratios are,

For Factor A: $\quad F = \dfrac{MS_A}{MS_{within}} = 15/3 = 5$

For Factor B: $\quad F = \dfrac{MS_B}{MS_{within}} = 5/3 = 1.67$

For AxB: $\quad F = \dfrac{MS_{AxB}}{MS_{within}} = 5/3 = 1.67$

Step 4: Make decision. The F-ratio for Factor A is in the critical region. Therefore, we reject this H_o and conclude that there is a significant difference between the mean for A1 and the mean for A2. The F-ratios for factor B and for the AxB interaction are not in the critical region. Therefore, we conclude that there is no significant main effect for factor B, and the data are not sufficient to conclude that there is an interaction between factors A and B.

HINTS AND CAUTIONS

1. You should note that several of the SS formulas in the two-factor ANOVA have the same basic structure. Recognizing this structure can make it much easier to learn the formulas. For example, three of the SS formulas are

computing variability due to differences between "things."
These "things" and the corresponding SS values are:

SS_A (between levels of factor A)

SS_B (between levels of factor B)

$SS_{bet\ cells}$ (between treatment conditions or cells)

The first term of each SS formula involves squaring a total and dividing by the number of scores that were added to compute the total. For example, SS_A squares each of the A totals and divides by bn which is the number of scores used to find each A total. The second term in each of these SS formulas is G^2/N. Thus, all three of these formulas have the same structure that was used to compute SS between treatments for the single-factor ANOVA:

$$SS_{between} = \Sigma \frac{T^2}{n} - \frac{G^2}{N}$$

Note: You also could consider SS_{total} as measuring differences between scores. In this case each score is its own total, and n = 1, so the formula for SS_{total} also fits this same general structure.

Also note that the degrees of freedom associated with each of these SS values can be determined by simply counting the number of "things" (or totals) and subtracting 1.

2. Remember that the F-ratios for factor A, factor B, and the AxB interaction can all have different values for df and therefore may have different critical values. Be sure that you use the appropriate critical region for each individual F-ratio.

1. In analysis of variance, an independent variable is called a
_____.

2. A two-factor analysis of variance involves three separate
hypothesis tests. (True or False)

3. In a two-factor ANOVA, a significant interaction means that
one of the factors has a significant effect but the second factor
does not. (True or False)

4. In a two-factor ANOVA, all of the F-ratios use the same
denominator (error term). (True or False)

5. If the F-ratios for factor A and factor B both have df = 1,
36, then the F-ratio for the interaction will also have df = 1,
36. (True or False)

6. If the F-ratios for factor A and factor B both have df = 2,
36, then the F-ratio for the interaction will also have df = 2,
36. (True or False)

7. In a line graph showing the means from a two-factor
experiment, if the lines are bent (not straight) then there is an
interaction between the two factors. (True or False)

8. In a two-factor ANOVA the value for $SS_{A \times B}$ is obtained by
subtracting SS_A and SS_B from $SS_{bet\ cells}$. (True or False)

9. For an experiment involving 3 levels of factor A and 4 levels
of factor B with a sample of n = 5 in each treatment condition,
    a.   What are the df values for the F-ratio for factor A?
    b.   What are the df values for the F-ratio for factor B?

c. What are the df values for the F-ratio for the interaction?

10. If a researcher expects that the difference between two treatment conditions will be greater for males than it is for females, then the researcher is predicting an <u>interaction</u> between the treatments and gender. (True or False)

11. Whenever a two-factor experiment results in a significant interaction, you should be cautious about interpreting the main effects because an interaction can distort, conceal, or exaggerate the main effects of the individual factors. (True or False)

Use the following data to answer questions 12 and 13. The data represent the means for each treatment condition in a two factor experiment. Note that one mean is not given.

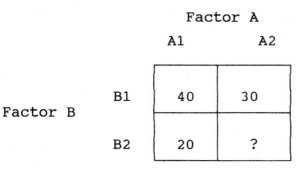

12. What value for the missing mean would result in no main effect for factor A?

13. What value for the missing mean would result in no interaction?

14. Use a two-factor analysis of variance to evaluate the following data from an independent-measures experimental

design using n = 5 subjects for each treatment condition (each cell). Use α = .05 for all tests.

	Factor B		
	B1	B2	B3
A1	$\bar{X} = 1$ AB = 5 SS = 15	$\bar{X} = 1$ AB = 5 SS = 15	$\bar{X} = 4$ AB = 20 SS = 25
A2	$\bar{X} = 1$ AB = 5 SS = 15	$\bar{X} = 3$ AB = 15 SS = 20	$\bar{X} = 8$ AB = 40 SS = 25

Factor A (row label)

$$N = 30$$
$$G = 90$$
$$\Sigma X^2 = 580$$

ANSWERS TO SELF-TEST

1.   In ANOVA an independent variable is called a factor.

2.   True

3.   False. The significance of the interaction is completely independent of the significance of the main effects.

4.   True

5.   True. $df_{A \times B} = df_A df_B = (1)(1) = 1$, and all three F-ratios have the same df value for the denominator.

6.   False. $df_{A \times B} = df_A df_B = (2)(2) = 4$. The F-ratio for the interaction would have df = 4, 36.

7.   False. An interaction exists if the lines in the graph are not parallel.

8. True

9. a. The F-ratio for factor A has df = 2, 48.
    b. The F-ratio for factor B has df = 3, 48.
    c. The F-ratio for the AxB interaction has df = 6, 48.

10. True. An interaction exists when the effect of one factor
(treatment) depends on the levels of the second factor (gender).

11. True

12. A mean of 30 would give both columns an overall mean of 30
which produces no main effect for factor A

13. A cell mean of 10 would produce no interaction. (In the top
row the mean decreases by 10 points from 40 to 30 as you move
from A1 to A2. To produce the same 10-point decrease in the
second row, the mean should drop from 20 to 10 as you move from
A1 to A2.)

14. The results of the two-factor ANOVA are summarized as
follows:

Source	SS	df	MS	
Between Cells	190	5		
Factor A	30	1	30	F(1, 24) = 6.00
Factor B	140	2	70	F(2, 24) = 14.00
AxB	20	2	10	F(2, 24) = 2.00
Within Cells	120	24	5	
Total	310	29		

For df = 1, 24 the critical value is 4.26. The F-ratio for
factor A is in the critical region so there is a significant
difference among the levels of factor A. With df = 2, 24 the
critical value is 3.40. The F-ratio for factor B is in the
critical region so there are significant differences among the
levels of factor B. The interaction is not significant.

CHAPTER 16

CORRELATION AND REGRESSION

A correlation is a statistical method used to measure and describe the relationship between two variables. A relationship exists when two variables vary together, as though they are linked. In general, correlational methods measure how much linkage there is. Do the variables always vary together? Sometimes vary together? Perhaps they vary independently of one another, in which case there is no relationship.

A correlation typically evaluates three aspects of the relationship: the direction, the form, and the degree of relationship. The most commonly used correlation is the Pearson correlation (r) which measures the direction and degree of linear relationship. Regression is a statistical procedure that determines the equation for the best-fitting straight line for a set of data. The equation is used to predict Y from a set of X values.

Usually, correlations are used in situations where a researcher is not attempting to manipulate either of the two variables, but rather is simply observing the both variables. To compute a correlation you need two scores, X and Y, for each individual in the sample. The Pearson correlation requires that the scores be numerical values on an interval or ratio scale of measurement. Other correlational methods exist for other scales of measurement.

   The Pearson correlation requires that you first measure the variability of X and Y scores separately by computing SS for the scores of each variable (SS_x and SS_y). Then, the covariability (tendency for X and Y to vary together) is measured by the sum of products (SP). The Pearson correlation is found by computing the ratio, $SP/\sqrt{(SS_x)(SS_y)}$. Thus the Pearson correlation is comparing the amount of covariability (variation from the relationship between X and Y) to the amount X and Y vary separately. The magnitude of the Pearson correlation ranges from 0 (indicating no linear relationship between X and Y) to 1.00 (indicating a perfect straight-line relationship between X and Y). The correlation can be either positive or negative depending on the direction of the relationship.

LEARNING OBJECTIVES

1.   Understand the Pearson correlation and what aspects of a relationship it measures.

2.   Know the uses and limitations of measures of correlation.

3.   Be able to compute the Pearson correlation by the regular formula (using either the definitional or computational formula for SP) or by the z-score formula.

4.   Be able to use a sample correlation to evaluate a hypothesis about the correlation for the general population.

5.   Recognize the circumstances where special correlations such as Spearman, point-biserial, and the phi-coefficient are used, and be able to compute these special correlations.

Chapter 16 - page 198

6.	Recognize the general form of a linear equation and be able to identify its slope and Y-intercept.

7.	Be able to compute the linear regression equation for a set of data.

8.	Be able to use the regression equation to compute a predicted value of Y for any given value of X.

NEW TERMS AND CONCEPTS

The following terms were introduced in this chapter. Define or describe each term and, where appropriate, describe how each term is related to other terms in the list.

positive relationship
negative relationship
perfect relationship
sum of products (of deviations)
Pearson correlation
restricted range
significance of a correlation
Spearman correlation
point-biserial correlation
phi-coefficient
coefficient of determination
linear relationship
linear equation
slope
Y-intercept
regression equation for Y
standard error of estimate

NEW FORMULAS

$$SP = \Sigma XY - \frac{(\Sigma X)(\Sigma Y)}{n} \quad \text{or} \quad SP = \Sigma (X - \bar{X})(Y - \bar{Y})$$

$$r = \frac{SP}{\sqrt{(SS_x)(SS_y)}}$$

$$\hat{Y} = bX + a \qquad b = \frac{SP}{SS_x} \qquad a = \bar{Y} - b\bar{X}$$

STEP BY STEP

The following example will be used to demonstrate the calculation of the Pearson correlation and the regression equation.

A researcher has pairs of scores (X and Y values) for a sample of n = 5 subjects. The data are as follows:

Person	X	Y
#1	0	-2
#2	2	-5
#3	8	14
#4	6	3
#5	4	0

Step 1: Sketch a scatterplot of the data and make a
preliminary estimate of the correlation. Also, sketch a
line through the middle of the data points and note the
slope and Y-intercept of the line.

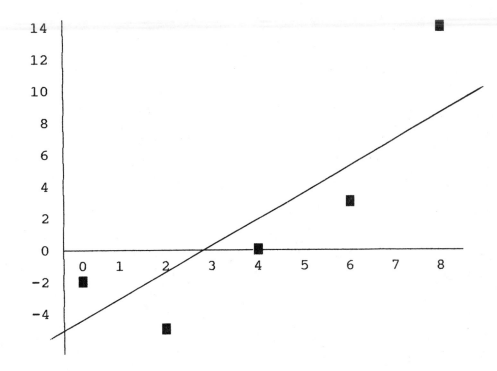

For these data, there appears to be a fairly good,
positive correlation - probably around r = +.7 or +.8. The
line has a positive slope and appears to intersect the
Y-axis about 5 points below zero.

Step 2: To compute the Pearson correlation you must find SS
for both X and Y as well as SP. These same values are
needed to find the regression equation. If both sets of
scores (X and Y) have means that are whole numbers, then you
may use the definitional formulas for SS and SP. Otherwise,
it is better to use the computational formulas. Although
these data have $\bar{X}$ = 4 and $\bar{Y}$ = 2, we will demonstrate the
computational formulas.

Using one large table, list the X and Y values in the first two columns, then continue with the squared values and the XY products. Find the sum of the numbers in each column. These sums are needed to find SS and SP.

X	Y	X^2	Y^2	XY
0	-2	0	4	0
2	-5	4	25	-10
8	14	64	196	112
6	3	36	9	18
4	0	16	0	0
(totals) 20	10	120	234	120

Use the sums from the table to compute SS for X and Y, and SP.

For X: $SS = \Sigma X^2 - \dfrac{(\Sigma X)^2}{n}$ $= 120 - \dfrac{20^2}{5}$

$= 120 - 80$

$= 40$

For Y: $SS = \Sigma Y^2 - \dfrac{(\Sigma Y)^2}{n}$ $= 234 - \dfrac{10^2}{5}$

$= 234 - 20$

$= 214$

and $SP = \Sigma XY - \dfrac{(\Sigma X)(\Sigma Y)}{n}$ $= 120 - \dfrac{(20)(10)}{5}$

$= 120 - 40$

$= 80$

Step 3: Compute the Pearson correlation and compare the answer with your preliminary estimate from Step 1. For these data,

$$r = \frac{SP}{\sqrt{(SS_x)(SS_y)}} = \frac{80}{\sqrt{(40)(214)}} = \frac{80}{92.52} = 0.865$$

The obtained correlation, r = +0.865 agrees with our preliminary estimate.

Step 4: Compute the values for the regression equation, and compare the obtained equation with the preliminary estimates made in Step 1. The general form of the regression equation is, Y = bX + a . For these data,

$$b = \frac{SP}{SS_x} = \frac{80}{40} = 2$$

and

$$a = \bar{Y} - b\bar{X}$$
$$= 2 - 2(4)$$
$$= -6$$

The regression equation is: $\hat{Y} = 2X - 6$

Both the slope constant (b = +2) and the Y-intercept (a = -6) agree with our preliminary estimates.

HINTS AND CAUTIONS

1. Remember, a correlation of -1.00 indicates a perfect fit, too. The sign indicates the direction of the relationship, not its magnitude.

2. Remember that n refers to the number of individuals (pairs of scores).

3. The formula for the Y-intercept (a) in the regression equation may be easier to remember if you note that this

formula simply guarantees that the point defined by $(\bar{X}, \bar{Y})$ is on the regression line. Thus, when $X = \bar{X}$, the predicted Y score will be $\bar{Y}$. In the equation,

$$\bar{Y} = b\bar{X} + a$$

Solving for this equation for the value of a yields,

$$a = \bar{Y} - b\bar{X}$$

4.   Remember that a regression equation should not be used to predict values outside the range of the original data.

=====

SELF-TEST AND REVIEW
=====

1.   Which of the following Pearson correlations shows the largest magnitude of relationship?

   a. -0.90   b. +0.74   c. +0.85   d. -0.33

2.   In a scatterplot, the more the data points vary from a straight line, the lower the value for the Pearson correlation. (True or False)

3.   When the standard error of estimate is large, accurate predictions can be made with the regression equation. (True or False)

4.   The strength of a correlation is measured by a numerical value ranging from 0 to 1.00. (True or False)

5.   In general, the more square-footage a person's home has, the greater the value of the car he/she drives. This demonstrates
   a.   a positive relationship
   b.   a negative relationship
   c.   a cause-effect relationship
   d.   all of the above

6. The Spearman correlation is computed from ranks for X and Y. (True or False)

7. The data for the point-biserial correlation are identical to the data used for
    a. the single-sample t statistic
    b. the independent-measures t statistic
    c. z-score hypothesis testing

8. Suppose that a sample of $n = 42$ pairs of X and Y scores yields a Pearson correlation of $r = +0.40$. Does this sample provide sufficient evidence to conclude that a significant correlation exists in the population? Test at the .05 level of significance, two tails.

9. Compute SP for the following sets of data. You should find that the definitional formula works well with Set I because both means are whole numbers. However, the computational formula is better with Set II where the means are fractions.

Data Set I		Data Set II	
X	Y	X	Y
1	5	1	0
5	2	4	4
6	9	3	1
15	20	2	1
8	4		

10. The book identified several points of caution when you are working with correlations.
    a. Describe the general problem associated with cause-and-effect relations.
    b. Describe the general problem associated with restricted range.

11.   A psychologist is examining the educational advantages of a preschool program. A sample of 24 fourth-grade children is obtained. Half of these children had attended preschool and the others had not. The psychologist records the scholastic achievement score for each child and obtains the following data:

Preschool			No Preschool		
8	6	8	8	5	7
9	7	7	6	8	5
6	9	8	7	5	6
9	7	8	7	5	6

Use a point-biserial correlation with the same data to measure the strength of the relation between preschool participation and scholastic achievement.

12.   A researcher would like to examine the relation between a person's sex and his or her preference between two brands of cola. The researcher suspects that women will prefer the sweeter cola and men will prefer the drier cola. A sample of 12 subjects is obtained. Of the 6 men in the sample, 5 prefer the drier cola. Of the 6 women, only 2 prefer the drier cola. Compute the phi-coefficient for these data to measure the relation between sex and preference.

13.   The general equation for expressing a linear relation between X and Y is, $Y = bX + a$
   a.   In this equation, what name and interpretation is given to the value of b?
   b.   What name and interpretation is given to the value of a?

14. For the linear equation, Y = 2X + 6, find the value of Y that corresponds to each of the following X values.

X	Y
0	
1	
10	
−3	

15. Find the regression equation for the following set of data.

X	Y
4	1
7	16
3	4
5	7
6	7

16. For the following set of scores
   a. Compute the Pearson correlation.
   b. Find the regression equation for predicting Y from X.

X	Y
0	16
1	6
2	9
3	0
4	9

1.   Choice a.   The larger the numerical value of the correlation the stronger the relationship.   The sign has nothing to do with strength.

2.   True.   Remember, the Pearson measures degree of linearity.

3.   False.   A large standard error of estimate indicates that there is a lot of error between the data points and the regression line.

4.   True.

5.   Choice a.

6.   True.

7.   Choice b.

8.   The null hypothesis states that there is no relationship in the population. H_o: $\rho = 0$
    With n = 42, the correlation must be greater than 0.304 to be significant.   This sample correlation is sufficient to conclude that there is a significant correlation in the population.

9.   For data set I, SP = 121.   For data set II, SP = 6.

10.   a.   A correlation between X and Y should not be interpreted
        as a cause-effect relationship.   Two variables can be
        related without one having a direct effect on the other.
        b.   With a restricted range you only see part of the
        relationship between X and Y.   You should not generalize a

correlation beyond the range of data for which it was
obtained.

11. Coding preschool as X = 0 and no-preschool as X = 1, gives
SS_x = 6, SS_y = 38.93, and SP = -8.50.   The point-biserial
correlation is r = -0.556.

12. Coding sex as the X variable with male = 0 and female = 1,
and coding preference as the Y variable with dry = 0 and sweet =
1, SS_x = 3, SS_y = 2.92, and SP = 1.50.   The phi-coefficient is
ϕ = 0.507.

13. a. In the linear equation, b is called the slope constant.
     This value determines how much Y changes when X is increased
     by 1 point.
     b. In the general linear equation, a is called the
     Y-intercept.   This is the value of Y when X = 0, and it
     determines the point where the line crosses (intercepts) the
     Y-axis.

14.

X	Y
0	6
1	8
10	26
-3	0

15. For these data, SS_x = 10 and SP = 30.   The regression
     equation is,
        $\hat{Y}$ = 3X - 8

16. a. SS_x = 10, SS_y = 134, and SP = -20.   The Pearson
     correlation is r = -0.546.
     b. The regression equation is, $\hat{Y}$ = -2X + 12.

CHAPTER 17

HYPOTHESIS TESTS WITH CHI-SQUARE

Chapter 17 introduces two non-parametric hypothesis tests using the chi-square statistic: the chi-square test for goodness of fit and the chi-square test for independence. The term "non-parametric" refers to the fact that the chi-square tests do not require assumptions about population parameters nor do they test hypotheses about population parameters. The most obvious difference between the chi-square tests and the other hypothesis tests we have considered (t and ANOVA) is the nature of the data. For chi-square, the data are frequencies rather than numerical scores.

The test for goodness-of-fit uses frequency data from a sample to test hypotheses about the shape or proportions of a population. Each individual in the sample is classified into one category on the scale of measurement. The data, called <u>observed frequencies</u>, simply count how many individuals from the sample are in each category. The null hypothesis specifies the proportion of the population that should be in each category.

The test for independence can be used and interpreted in two different ways:

1. Testing hypotheses about the relationship between two variables in a population, or

2. Testing hypotheses about differences between population proportions.

Although the two versions of the test for independence appear to be different, they are equivalent and they are interchangeable. The first version of the test emphasizes the relation between chi-square and a correlation because both procedures examine the relationship between two variables. The second version of the test emphasizes the relation between chi-square and an independent-measures t test (or ANOVA) because both tests use data from two (or more) samples to test hypotheses about two (or more) populations.

The first version of the chi-square test for independence requires one sample where each individual is classified on two different variables. The data are usually presented in a matrix with the categories for one variable defining the rows and the categories of the second variable defining the columns. The data, called observed frequencies, simply show how many individuals from the sample are in each cell of the matrix. The null hypothesis for this test states that there is no relationship between the two variables; that is, the two variables are independent.

The second version of the test for independence requires a separate sample for each population being compared. The same variable is measured for each sample by classifying individual subjects into categories of the variable. The data are presented in a matrix with the different samples defining the rows and the categories of the variable defining the columns. The data, again called observed frequencies, show how many individuals are in each cell of the matrix. The null hypothesis for this test states that the proportions (the distribution across categories) are the same for all of the populations.

The calculation of the chi-square statistic require two steps:

1) The null hypothesis is used to construct an idealized sample distribution of <u>expected frequencies</u> that describes how the sample would look if the data were in perfect agreement with the null hypothesis.

For the goodness of fit test, the expected frequency for each category is obtained by

$$\text{expected frequency} = f_e = pn$$

where p is the proportion from the null hypothesis and n is the size of the sample.

For the test for independence, the expected frequency for each cell in the matrix is obtained by

$$\text{expected frequency} = f_e = \frac{(\text{row total})(\text{column total})}{n}$$

2) A chi-square statistic is computed to measure the amount of discrepancy between the ideal sample (expected frequencies from H_o) and the actual sample data (the observed frequencies = f_o). A large discrepancy results in a large value for chi-square and indicates that the data do not fit the null hypothesis and the hypothesis should be rejected. The calculation of chi-square is the same for all chi-square tests:

$$\text{chi-square} = \Sigma \frac{(f_o - f_e)^2}{f_e}$$

The fact that chi-square tests do not require scores from an interval or ratio scale makes these tests a valuable alternative to the t tests, ANOVA, or correlation because they can be used with data measured on a nominal or an ordinal scale.

1. Recognize the experimental situations where a chi-square tests is appropriate.

2. Be able to conduct a chi-square test for goodness of fit to evaluate a hypothesis about the shape of a population frequency distribution.

3. Be able to conduct a chi-square test for independence to evaluate a hypothesis about the relationship between two variables.

NEW TERMS AND CONCEPTS

The following terms were introduced in this chapter. Define or describe each term and, where appropriate, describe how each term is related to other terms in the list.

    parametric statistical tests
    non-parametric statistical tests
    expected frequencies
    observed frequencies
    chi-square statistic
    chi-square distribution
    chi-square test for goodness of fit
    chi-square test for independence

$$\chi^2 = \Sigma \frac{(f_o - f_e)^2}{f_e}$$

$$f_e = pn \qquad \text{(test for goodness of fit)}$$

$$f_e = \frac{(\text{Row Total})(\text{Column Total})}{n} \qquad \text{(test for independence)}$$

STEP BY STEP

The chi-square test for independence. The chi-square test for independence uses frequency data to test a hypothesis about the relationship between two variables. The null hypothesis states that the two variables are independent (no relation). Rejecting H_o indicates that the data provide convincing evidence of a consistent relation between the two variables. The following example will be used to demonstrate this chi-square test.

A psychologist would like to examine preferences for the different seasons of the year and how these preferences are related to gender. A sample of 200 people is obtained and the individuals are classified by sex and preference. The psychologist would like to know if there is a consistent relationship between sex and preference. The frequency data are as follows:

Favorite Season

	Summer	Fall	Winter	Spring
Males	28	32	15	45
Females	23	8	5	35

Step 1: State the hypotheses and select an alpha level. The null hypothesis says that there is no relationship.

H_o: Preference is independent of sex. One version of the null hypothesis states that there is no relationship between preference and sex. The second version of H_o states that there is no difference between the distribution of preferences for males and the distribution of preferences for females (both distributions have the same proportions).

The alternative hypothesis simply says that the two variables are not independent.

H_1: Preference is related to sex, or the distribution of preferences is different for males and females.
We will use $\alpha = .05$

Step 2: Locate the critical region. The degrees of freedom for the chi-square test for independence are

$$df = (C - 1)(R - 1)$$

For this example, df = 3(1) = 3. Sketch the distribution and locate the extreme 5%. The critical boundary is 7.81.

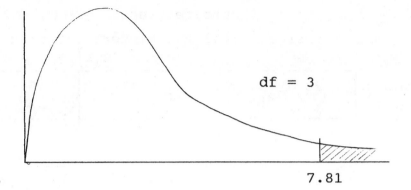

df = 3

7.81

Step 3: Compute the test statistic. The major concern for this chi-square test is determining the expected frequencies. We begin with a blank matrix showing only the row and column totals from the data.

Favorite Season

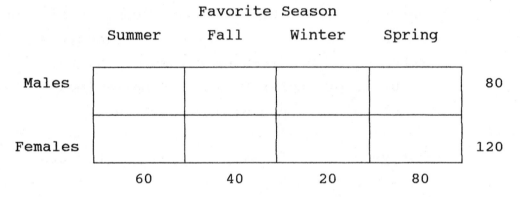

	Summer	Fall	Winter	Spring	
Males					80
Females					120
	60	40	20	80	

The expected frequencies are determined by the null hypothesis. In this example, H_o says that the distribution of preferences is the same for both genders. Therefore, we must determine the "distribution of preferences."

For the total sample of n = 200 the data show:

$60/200 = 30\%$ prefer Summer

$40/200 = 20\%$ prefer Fall

$20/200 = 10\%$ prefer Winter

$80/200 = 40\%$ prefer Spring

Next, we apply this distribution to each sex group.
There are 120 males. Using the proportions from the overall distribution, we would expect,

        30% of 120 = 36 males prefer summer
        20% of 120 = 24 males prefer fall
        10% of 120 = 12 males prefer winter
        40% of 120 = 48 males prefer spring

For the group of 80 females we would expect

        30% of 80 = 24 females prefer summer
        20% of 80 = 16 females prefer fall
        10% of 80 =   8 females prefer winter
        40% of 80 = 32 females prefer spring

Place these values in a matrix of expected frequencies.

Favorite Season

	Summer	Fall	Winter	Spring	
Males	36	24	12	48	80
Females	24	16	8	32	120
	60	40	20	80	

Now you are ready to compute the chi-square statistic.
a)   For each cell in the matrix, find the difference between the expected and the observed frequency.
b)   Square the difference.
c)   Divide the squared difference by the expected frequency.
d)   Sum the resulting values for each category

f_o	f_e	$(f_o - f_e)$	$(f_o - f_e)^2$	$(f_o - f_e)^2/f_e$
28	36	8	64	1.78
32	24	8	64	2.67
15	12	3	9	0.75
45	48	3	9	0.19
32	24	8	64	2.67
8	16	8	64	4.00
5	8	3	9	1.13
35	32	3	9	0.28
				$13.47 = \chi^2$

Step 4: Make decision. The chi-square value is in the critical region. Therefore, we reject H_o and conclude that there is a significant relation between sex and preferred season.

To describe the nature of the relationship, you can compare the data with the expected frequencies. From this comparison it should be clear that more men prefer fall and more women prefer summer than would be expected by chance.

HINTS AND CAUTIONS

1. When computing expected frequencies for either chi-square test, it is wise to check your arithmetic by being certain that $\Sigma f_e = \Sigma f_o = n$. In the test for independence, the expected frequencies in any row or column should sum to the same total as the corresponding row or column in the observed frequencies.

2.   Whenever a chi-square test has df = 1, the difference
      (absolute value) between f_o and f_e will be the same for
      every category. This is true for either the goodness of fit
      test with 2 categories, or the test of independence with 4
      categories. Knowing this fact can help you check the
      calculation of expected frequencies and it can simplify the
      calculation of the chi-square statistic.

SELF-TEST AND REVIEW

1. In a chi-square test, the sample data are called <u>observed</u>
<u>frequencies</u>. (True or False)

2. One advantage of the chi-square tests is that they can be
used when the data are measured on a nominal scale. (True or
False)

3. The chi-square test for independence requires that each
individual be categorized on two separate variables. (True or
False)

4. The df value for a chi-square test does <u>not</u> depend on the
sample size. (True or False)

5. In a chi-square test, it is possible for the observed
frequencies to be fractions or decimal values. (True or False)

6. In general, a large value for chi-square will tend to reject
the null hypothesis. (True or False)

7. A chi-square statistic can never have a value less than zero.
(True or False)

8. For a chi-square test for goodness of fit, if H_o predicts no preference among five brands of pizza, what would be the expected frequencies for a sample of n = 60 individuals?

9. For a chi-square test for goodness of fit, if H_o predicts that women outnumber men by 3 to 1 in the nursing profession, what would be the expected frequencies for a sample of n = 60 nurses? (Hint: a 3 to 1 ratio means that out of every four nurses, three are women and one is a man.)

10. For the chi-square test for goodness of fit,
   a. What is the value of df for a test with four categories and a sample of n = 100?
   b. What is the value of df for a test with four categories and a sample of n = 1000?
   c. If a researcher reports a chi-square statistic with df = 5, how many categories are in the distribution?

11. A researcher is testing four new flavors of bubble gum using a sample that consists of 50 men, 200 women, and 250 children. Each individual selects his/her favorite flavor. In the total sample of 500 people, 100 selected Flavor A, 200 chose B, 150 picked C, and only 50 preferred D.
   a. If these data are used for a chi-square test for independence, state the null hypothesis.
   b. Use the matrix below to fill in the expected frequencies for the chi-square test for independence.

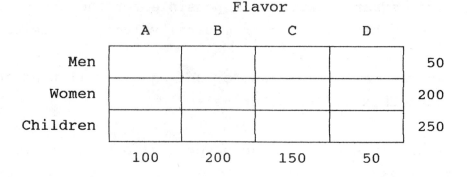

12. A researcher is interested in the relationship between birth order and personality. A sample of n = 100 people is obtained, all of whom grew up in families as one of three children. Each person is given a personality test and the researcher also records the person's birth order position (1st born, 2nd, or 3rd). The frequencies from this study are shown in the following table. On the basis of these data can the researcher conclude that there is a significant relation between birth order and personality? Test at the .05 level of significance.

Birth Position

	1st	2nd	3rd
Outgoing	13	31	16
Reserved	17	19	4

ANSWERS TO SELF-TEST

1. True

2. True

3. True

4. True

5. False. Observed frequencies are actual counts of how many individuals are in each category. These are always whole numbers.

6.   True.   A large value for chi-square indicates a large discrepancy between the observed frequencies (data) and the expected frequencies (from H_o).

7.   True.   Chi-square is computed by summing squared values (always positive).

8.   The null hypothesis specifies equal proportions for all 5 categories.   With n = 60, the expected frequencies will all be f_e = 12.

9.   The expected frequencies are f_e = 45 women and f_e = 15 men.

10.   a.   df = 3
     b.   df = 3   (df is determined by the number of categories, not by the number of subjects)
     c.   With df = 5, there would be 6 categories.

11.   a.   One version of the null hypothesis states that gum preference is independent of the age/gender classifications.   The second version of H_o states that the distribution of flavor preferences is the same (same proportions) for men, women, and children.

b.

Flavor

	A	B	C	D	
Men	10	20	15	5	50
Women	40	80	60	20	200
Children	50	100	75	25	250
	100	200	150	50	

12.   The null hypothesis states that there is no relation between
birth order and personality - the two variables are independent.
With df = 2, the critical value for this test is 5.99.   The
expected frequencies are as follows:

                         Birth Position
                  1st   2nd   3rd

	1st	2nd	3rd
Outgoing	18	30	12
Reserved	12	20	8

For these data, the chi-square statistic is 6.89.   Reject H_o
and conclude that there is a significant relation between
personality and birth order.

CHAPTER 18

THE BINOMIAL TEST

CHAPTER SUMMARY

The binomial test introduced in Chapter 18 provides a method for testing hypotheses about population proportions for populations consisting of binomial data. Binomial data exist when the measurement procedure classifies individuals into exactly two distinct categories. Traditionally, the two categories are identified as A and B, and the population proportions are identified as $p(A) = p$ and $p(B) = q$. The null hypothesis specifies the values of p and q for the population. For example, when testing for an unbalanced coin, the null hypothesis would state that the coin is balanced or, $p(Heads) = p = .50$, and $p(Tails) = q = .50$.

The sample data for the binomial test consist of a set of n individuals who are classified in categories A and B. The sample statistic, X, is simply the number of individuals classified in category A. The logic underlying the binomial test is identical to the logic for the original z-score test (Chapter 8) or the t-statistic hypothesis tests (Chapters 9, 10, and 11). The test statistic compares the sample data with the hypothesized value for the population. If the data are consistent with the hypothesis, we conclude that the hypothesis is reasonable. However, if there is a large discrepancy between the data and the hypothesis, we reject the hypothesis.

When the values of pn and qn are both greater than or equal to 10, the binomial distribution is approximately normal (see Chapter 6) and the test is conducted using a z-score for the test statistic and the unit normal table to determine critical values.

The sign test is a special application of the binomial test used to evaluate the results from a related-samples research design comparing two treatment conditions. The difference score for each individual is classified as either an increase (+) or a decrease (−) and the binomial test evaluates a null hypothesis stating that increases and decreases are equally likely: $p(+) = p(-) = 1/2$.

LEARNING OBJECTIVES

---

1. Recognize binomial data and identify situations where a binomial test is appropriate.

2. Understand the criteria that must be satisfied before the binomial distribution is normal and the z-score statistic can be used.

3. Be able to perform all of the necessary computations for the binomial test.

4. Recognize when a sign test is appropriate and be able to perform the necessary computations.

NEW TERMS AND CONCEPTS

The following terms were introduced in this chapter. Define or describe each term and, where appropriate, describe how each term is related to other terms in the list.

    binomial data
    binomial distribution
    binomial test
    sign test

NEW FORMULAS

$$z = \frac{X - pn}{\sqrt{npq}} \qquad z = \frac{X/n - p}{\sqrt{pq/n}}$$

STEP BY STEP

The Binomial Hypothesis Test: The binomial test presented in this chapter is used to test a hypothesis about unknown population proportions using binomial data from a single sample. Interpretation of the z-score statistic requires that the values of pn and qn are both at least 10. The binomial test uses the same four-step procedure that we use for all hypothesis tests. We will use the following example to demonstrate the binomial test.

A survey of last year's graduating college seniors showed that 40% intended to continue their education with some form of graduate training. In a sample of n = 54 seniors from this year's class only X = 10 indicated that they planned to go on for graduate training. On the basis of this sample can you conclude that this year's class has significantly different plans than last year's class? Test at the .05 level of significance.

Step 1: State Hypotheses and select an alpha level. The null hypothesis states that the proportions for this year's class are not different from last year's class.

H_o: p = p(continue education) = 0.40 (no change)

H_1: p ≠ 0.40 (this year's proportion is different)

For this example we are using α = .05

Step 2: Locate the critical region. For this example pn = 0.40(54) = 21.6 and qn = 0.60(54) = 32.4. Both values are greater than 10 so the normal approximation is appropriate. For a two-tailed test with α = .05 the critical z-score values are z = ±1.96.

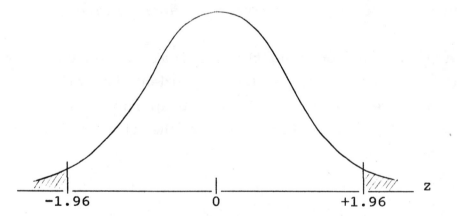

Step 3: Compute the test statistic: For this sample we have X = 10. Using n = 54 and the hypothesized values of p = 0.40 and q = 0.60 from H_o, the z-score statistic is

$$z = \frac{X - pn}{\sqrt{npq}} = \frac{10 - (0.40)(54)}{\sqrt{54(0.4)(0.6)}} = \frac{10 - 21.6}{3.6}$$

$$= -3.222$$

Step 4: Make decision. The z-score we obtained is in the critical region. This is a very unlikely value to obtain by chance (p < .05). Therefore, we reject H_o and conclude that these data provide sufficient evidence to demonstrate that this year's graduating class has significantly different proportions than last year's class.

HINTS AND CAUTIONS

1. Remember, the values of pn and qn must <u>both</u> be greater than or equal to 10 before the z-score normal approximation can be used.

2. When you are discarding zero differences with the sign test, remember to reduce the value of n appropriately.

3. Be careful when locating the critical region using the unit normal table. The table does not identify critical values for two-tailed tests. To find the appropriate critical value, you must look for one-half the alpha value in column C of the table.

SELF-TEST AND REVIEW

1. For the sign test, it is more conservative to include the zero differences in the analysis. (True or False)

2. In the binomial test, p must be equal q because there are only two events possible. (True or False)

3.   The mean of the normal approximation to the binomial distribution is $\mu = pn$.   (True or False)

4.   The binomial test most resembles
    a.   analysis of variance
    b.   a test comparing two population means
    c.   the chi square test for goodness of fit

5.   In a blind taste test of two leading brands of herbal tea, 25 out of 36 people preferred brand A.   Do these data indicate a significant preference for brand A over brand B?   Test at the .05 level of significance.

6.   According to most estimates, 10% of the general population are left-handed and 90% are right-handed.   A neurological theory of handedness and cerebral dominance predicts that there should be a disproportionate number of left-handers among artists.   For a sample of $n = 150$ artists, a psychologist finds that 24 are left-handed.   Is there a higher proportion of left-handers among artist than there is for the general population?   Test with alpha set at .05.

7.   An instructor is curious if students cut more or fewer classes in the second half of the semester than in the first half.   For a sample of $n = 38$ students, the instructor records the number of classes each student missed up to midterm and then how many each missed from midterm to the end of the semester. Twenty four students showed an increase in cuts from the first half to the second half of the semester, 12 showed a decrease, and 2 showed no change.   Are significantly more classes cut in one part of the semester than the other?   Test with $\alpha = .05$.

8.   A test for ESP requires a subject to predict the suit of a playing card randomly selected from a complete deck. If the test involves a series of n = 40 predictions, how many would a subject need to predict correctly to do significantly better than chance. Assume a two-tailed test with α = .05.

9.   In the binomial test, like most hypothesis tests, the amount of error that is expected between a sample and its population depends on the size of the sample. In general, the bigger the sample, the less error there should be. This phenomenon is demonstrated with the following examples:

   a.   In the general population of newborn babies, males and females are equally likely. In the month of July a local hospital records n = 25 births of which 60% are males. Is this result significantly different from what would be expected by chance? Test with α = .05.

   b.   Suppose that the hospital had n = 100 births of which 60% were males. Is this result significantly different from chance? Again, test with α = .05.

   c.   Explain why one result is significant and the other is not.

10.   A company embarks on a new program to boost morale and improve employee productivity. Records for a sample of n = 64 employees indicate that 39 showed improved productivity after the program was initiated, and 46 reported improved morale.

   a.   Do these data indicate that the program had a significant effect on productivity? Test at the .01 level of significance.

   b.   Do the data indicate a significant effect on morale? Again, test at the .01 level of significance.

11. Upon enrolling in State University, freshmen are required to take an English placement exam. Over the past several years, 20% of the new students have failed the test and have been placed in remedial classes. In a sample of n = 100 students from this year's class, only 12 failed the test. Do these data indicate a significant change from previous years? Test at the .05 level of significance.

===========

ANSWERS TO SELF-TEST

===========

1. True. The most conservative way to handle zero differences is to assign half of the zero to the positive differences and half to the negative differences.

2. False. Consider the example in the Step-by-Step section. There are two possible events (graduate school or no graduate school), but p does not equal q.

3. True.

4. Choice c. A chi-square test for goodness of fit with two categories is like the binomial test. Both start out with hypotheses about population proportions.

5. H_o: $p = q = 1/2$ (no preference). X = 25 out of 36 corresponds to z = 2.33. Reject H_o and conclude that there is a significant preference for brand A.

6. H_o: $p = 0.1$ left-handed and $q = 0.9$ right-handed. X = 24 out of 150 corresponds to z = 2.45. Reject H_o and conclude that there is a significant difference in the proportion of left-handers among artists.

7. H_o: p = q = 1/2 (increases and decreases are equally likely). Discarding the 2 students who showed no difference leaves n = 36. X = 24 out of 36 corresponds to z = 2.00. Reject H_o and conclude that there is a significant difference between the two halves of the semester.

8.   With α = .05, the subject must have a z-score greater than 1.96 to be significantly better than chance. By chance, you would expect p = 1/4 correct and q = 3/4 incorrect predictions. With n = 40, the standard error is $\sqrt{npq} = \sqrt{40(/1/4)(3/4)}$ = 2.74. The subject must be above chance by at least 2.74(1.96) = 5.37 to be in the critical region. With a chance level of (1/4)(40) = 10, the subject must get at least X = 15.37 (X = 16) to be significantly better than chance.

9.   a. H_o: p = q = 1/2 (males and females are equally likely. 60% of n = 25 is X = 15 which corresponds to z = 1.00. Fail to reject the null hypothesis. These data do not indicate a significant difference from chance.
      b. With n = 100, 60% males is X = 60. This value corresponds to z = 2.00. Reject H_o and conclude that this is significantly different from chance.
      c. Both samples have 60% males. However, with n = 25 the discrepancy between the actual number of males (X = 15) and the hypothesized proportion is not sufficient to be significant. With n = 100, the discrepancy between the actual number (X =60) and the hypothesized proportion is large enough to be significant.

10.. a. H_o: p = q = 1/2 (increases and decreases are equally likely. The sample value, X = 39, corresponds to z = 1.75. Fail to reject H_o and conclude that these data are not sufficient to conclude that there has been a significant change in productivity.

b. H_o: $p = q = 1/2$ (increases and decreases are equally likely. The sample value, X = 46, corresponds to z = 3.50. Reject H_o and conclude that these data are sufficient to conclude that there has been a significant change in employee morale.

11. H_o: $p = 0.2$ fail and $q = 0.8$ pass. The sample value, X = 12, corresponds to z = -2.00. Reject the null hypothesis and conclude that the proportions for this year's class are significantly different from last year.

CHAPTER 19

STATISTICAL METHODS FOR ORDINAL DATA

CHAPTER SUMMARY

Chapter 19 introduces three statistical techniques that have been developed specifically for use with ordinal data; that is, data where the measurement procedure simply arranges the subjects into a rank-ordered sequence. The statistical methods presented in this chapter can be used when the original data consist of ordinal measurements (ranks), or when the original data come from an interval or ratio scale but are converted to ranks because they do not satisfy the assumptions of a standard parametric test such as the t statistic. Three statistical methods are introduced:

1. The Mann-Whitney test evaluates the difference between two treatments or two populations using data from an independent-measures design; that is, two separate samples.

2. The Wilcoxon test evaluates the difference between two treatment conditions using data from a repeated-measures design; that is, the same sample is tested/measured in both treatment conditions.

3. The Spearman correlation is used to measure the degree
and direction of relationship between two ordinal-scale
variables.

THE MANN-WHITNEY U TEST

The Mann-Whitney test can be viewed as an alternative to the
independent-measures t test (Chapter 10). The test uses the data
from two separate samples to test for a significant difference
between two treatments or two populations. However, the Mann-
Whitney test only requires that you are able to rank order the
individual scores; there is no need to compute means or
variances. The null hypothesis for the Mann-Whitney test simply
states that there is no systematic or consistent difference
between the two treatments (populations) being compared. The
calculation of the Mann-Whitney U statistic requires:

1. Combine the two samples and rank order the individuals
in the combined group.

2. Once the complete set is rank ordered, you can compute
the Mann-Whitney U by either
     a. Find the sum of the ranks for each of the original
     samples, and use the formula to compute a U statistic
     for each sample.

     b. Compute a score for each sample by viewing the
     ranked data (1st, 2nd, etc.) as if they were finishing
     positions in a race. Each subject in sample A receives
     one point for every individual from sample B that
     he/she beats. The total number of points is the U
     statistic for sample A. In the same way, a U statistic
     is computed for sample B.

3. The Mann-Whitney U is the smaller of the two U
statistics computed for the samples.

If there is a consistent difference between the two treatments, the two samples should be distributed at opposite ends of the rank ordering. In this case, the final U value should be small. At the extreme, when there is no overlap between the two samples, you will obtain U = 0. Thus, a small value for the Mann-Whitney U indicates a difference between the treatments. To determine whether the obtained U value is sufficiently small to be significant, you must consult the Mann-Whitney table. For large samples, the obtained U statistic can be converted to a z-score and the critical region can be determined using the unit normal table.

THE WILCOXON T TEST

The Wilcoxon test can be viewed as an alternative to the repeated-measures t test (Chapter 11). The test uses the data from one sample where each individual has been observed in two different treatment conditions to test for a significant difference between the two treatments. However, the Wilcoxon test only requires that you are able to rank order the difference scores; there is no need to measure how much difference exists for each subject, or to compute a mean or variance for the difference scores. The null hypothesis for the Wilcoxon test simply states that there is no systematic or consistent difference between the two treatments being compared. The calculation of the Wilcoxon T statistic requires:

1. Observe the difference between treatment 1 and treatment 2 for each subject.

2. Rank order the absolute size of the differences without regard to sign (positive = increase and negative = decrease).

3. Find the sum of the ranks for the positive differences and the sum of the ranks for the negative differences.

4. The Wilcoxon T is the smaller of the two sums.

If there is a consistent difference between the two treatments, the difference scores should be consistently positive (or consistently negative). At the extreme, all the differences will be in the same direction and one of the two sums will be zero. (If there are no negative differences then ΣRanks = 0 for the negative differences.) Thus, a small value for T indicates a difference between treatments. To determine whether the obtained T value is sufficiently small to be significant, you must consult the Wilcoxon table.

THE SPEARMAN CORRELATION

The Spearman correlation can be viewed as an alternative to the Pearson correlation. However, the Pearson correlation measures the degree and direction of <u>linear</u> relationship and the Spearman correlation simply measures the degree and direction of relationship <u>independent of the specific form</u>. Thus, the Spearman correlation can be used when a researcher is not concerned about the exact form of the relationship but simply wants to evaluate the consistency of the relationship. The calculation of the Spearman correlation requires:

1. Two variables are observed for each individual.

2. The observations for each variable are rank ordered. Note that the X values and the Y values are ranked separately.

3. After the variables have been ranked, the Spearman correlation is computed by either:

    a. Using the Pearson formula with the ranked data.

    b. Using the special Spearman formula (assuming there are few, if any, tied ranks).

LEARNING OBJECTIVES

1. Know when the Mann-Whitney U and the Wilcoxon Signed-Ranks tests are appropriate.

2. Be able to compute and evaluate the Mann-Whitney U and the Wilcoxon T.

3. Understand the Spearman correlation and how it differs from the Pearson correlation in terms of the data it uses and the type of relationship it measures.

NEW TERMS AND CONCEPTS

The following terms were introduced in this chapter. Define or describe each term and, where appropriate, describe how each term is related to other terms in the list.

ordinal data

Mann-Whitney U

normal approximation to the Mann-Whitney U

Wilcoxon T

Spearman correlation

monotonic relation

NEW FORMULAS

$$U_A = n_A n_B + \frac{n_A(n_A + 1)}{2} - \Sigma R_A$$

$$U_B = n_A n_B + \frac{n_B(n_B + 1)}{2} - \Sigma R_B$$

$$U_A + U_B = n_A n_B$$

$$z = \frac{U - \dfrac{n_A n_B}{2}}{\sqrt{\dfrac{n_A n_B(n_A + n_B + 1)}{12}}}$$

$$\text{Spearman } r_s = 1 - \frac{6\Sigma D^2}{n(n^2 - 1)}$$

STEP BY STEP

The Mann-Whitney U test: As a non-parametric alternative to the independent-measures t, the Mann-Whitney test uses the data from two separate samples to test hypotheses about the difference between two populations or two treatments. The following example will be used to demonstrate the Mann-Whitney U test.

A researcher obtains two random samples with n = 5 in one sample and n = 6 in the other. Treatment A is administered to

the first sample and the second sample gets Treatment B. The
resulting scores for the two samples are:

Sample A: 15, 12, 9, 19, 20
Sample B: 8, 10, 5, 14, 3, 6

Step 1: State the hypotheses and select an alpha level. The
hypotheses for the Mann-Whitney U are stated in general
terms and do not concern any specific population parameters.

H_o: There is no systematic difference between the two
         treatments.

H_1:   There is a systematic difference that causes
         the scores from one sample to be generally
         higher than the scores from the other sample.

We will use $\alpha = .05$.

Step 2: Locate the critical region. For the Mann-
Whitney test, a small value of U indicates a substantial
difference between the two samples. To determine the
critical value, you must consult the Mann-Whitney table.
With n = 5 and n = 6 for the two samples, and with $\alpha = .05$,
the critical value is U = 3. If the data produce U = 3 or
smaller we will conclude that there is a significant
difference between the two treatments.

Step 3: Compute the test statistic. Although the Mann-
Whitney U does not require much calculation, there are
several steps involved in finding the U value.

a. Combine the two samples and list all the scores in
rank-order from smallest to largest.

b. For each individual in sample A, count how many of
the scores from sample B have lower positions in the
list. Sum these values for all the individuals in
sample A. This is U_A.

c. In the same way, find U_B.

d. The Mann-Whitney U is the smaller of the two U values.

For these data:

Rank	1	2	3	4	5	6	7	8	9	10	11
Score	3	5	6	8	9	10	12	14	15	19	20
Sample	B	B	B	B	A	B	A	B	A	A	A
					:		:		:	:	:
Points for					:		:		:	:	:
Sample A					2		1		0	0	0

Sample A has a U value of $U_A = 2 + 1 = 3$

Using the same procedure, compute U for sample B. To check your calculations be sure that

$$U_A + U_B = n_A n_B$$

You should find that the smaller U is U = 3.

Step 4: Make decision. The U value of U = 3 is in the critical region. This is a very unlikely value to obtain by chance, so we reject H_o and conclude that there is a systematic difference between the two treatments.

The Wilcoxon test: As a non-parametric alternative to the repeated-measures t, the Wilcoxon test uses data from a single sample measured in two treatment conditions. The difference scores for the sample are used to test a hypothesis about the difference between the treatments in the population. The following example will be used to demonstrate the Wilcoxon T test.

A researcher obtains a random sample of n = 7 individuals and tests each person in two different treatment conditions. The data for this sample are,

Subject	Treatment 1	Treatment 2	Difference
#1	8	24	+16
#2	12	10	− 2
#3	15	19	+ 4
#4	31	52	+21
#5	26	20	− 6
#6	32	40	+ 8
#7	19	29	+10

Step 1: State the hypotheses and select an alpha level. The hypotheses for the Wilcoxon test do not refer to any specific population parameter.

H_o: There is no systematic difference between the two treatments.

H_1: There is a consistent difference between the treatments that causes the scores in one treatment to be generally higher than the scores in the other treatment.

We will use α = .05.

Step 2: Locate the critical region. A small value for the Wilcoxon T indicates that the difference scores were consistently positive (or consistently negative) which indicates a systematic treatment difference. Thus, small values will tend to refute H_o. To locate the critical value, consult the Wilcoxon table with n = 7 and α = .05. For these data a Wilcoxon T of 2 or smaller is needed to reject H_o.

Step 3:   Compute the test statistic.   The calculation of the
Wilcoxon T is very simple, but requires several stages.
     a.   Ignoring the signs (+ or -), rank the difference
     scores from smallest to largest.

     b.   Compute the sum of the ranks for the positive
     differences and the sum for the negative
     differences.

     c.   The Wilcoxon T is the smaller of the two sums.

For these data,

Difference		Rank		
(+)	16	6		
(-)	2	1		
(+)	4	2	ΣR_+	= 24
(+)	21	7		
(-)	6	3	ΣR_-	= 4
(+)	8	4	The Wilcoxon T = 4	
(+)	10	5		

Step 4:   Make decision.   The obtained T value is not in the
critical region.   These data are not significantly different
from chance.   Therefore, we fail to reject H_o and conclude
that there is not sufficient evidence to conclude that there
is a systematic difference between the two treatments.

Spearman Correlation: The Spearman correlation measures the
degree of relationship between two variables that are both
measured on ordinal scales.   If the original data are from
interval or ratio scales, you can rank the scores, then compute
the Spearman correlation.   The following data will be used to
demonstrate the calculation of the Spearman correlation.

X	Y	
5	12	
7	18	(Both X and Y are measured on
2	9	interval scales)
15	14	
10	13	

Step 1: Check that the X values and the Y values consist of ranks (ordinal data). If not, rank the X's and rank the Y's. Caution: Rank X and Y separately.

For these data,

X Score	X Rank	Y Rank	Y Score
5	2	2	12
7	3	5	18
2	1	1	9
15	5	4	14
10	4	3	13

Step 2: To use the special Spearman formula, compute the difference (D) between the X rank and the Y rank for each individual. Also, find the squared difference (D^2) and the sum of the squared differences.

(Note: The signs of the difference scores are unimportant because you are squaring each D.)

X Rank	Y Rank	D	D^2
2	2	0	0
3	5	2	4
1	1	0	0
5	4	1	1
4	3	1	1
		6	$= \Sigma D^2$

Step 3:   Substitute ΣD^2 and n in the Spearman formula.

$$r_s = 1 - \frac{6\Sigma D^2}{n(n^2 - 1)}$$

$$= 1 - \frac{6(6)}{5(25 - 1)}$$

$$= 1 - \frac{36}{120}$$

$$= 0.70$$

There is a positive relation between X and Y for these data. The correlation is fairly high (although not perfect) which indicates a very consistent positive relation.

HINTS AND CAUTIONS

1.   Sometimes it is obvious from looking at the data which sample has the smaller Mann-Whitney U value. Nevertheless, it is wise to compute both U values and check your computations by the formula, $U_A + U_B = n_A n_B$

2.   Remember, to be significant the Mann-Whitney U and the Wilcoxon T must be equal to or less than the critical value provided in the table. This is different from most statistical tests where a large value indicates significance.

3. In computing the Wilcoxon T, it is important to remember that the signs should be ignored when ranking the difference scores.

4. The special formula for the Spearman correlation often causes trouble. Remember, the value of the fraction is computed separately and then subtracted from 1.00. The 1 is not a part of the fraction.

====================
SELF-TEST AND REVIEW
====================

1. One limitation of ordinal measurements is that they do not determine how much difference there is between two individuals. (True or False)

2. When ranking existing scores, it often is necessary to find ranks for tied scores. Demonstrate this process by assigning ranks to the following scores.
   Scores: 3, 8, 8, 10, 14, 14, 14, 27, 35, 100

3. A Mann-Whitney T of zero indicates that there is no significant difference between the two treatments being compared. (True or False)

4. In the following data, two samples (A and B) have been combined and rank-ordered. Find the U value for each of the two samples.

Rank	Sample
1	A
2	A
3	B
4	A
5	B
6	A
7	A
8	B
9	B
10	A

5.   A psychologist performs a study to assess the effect of meaning on memory. One sample of subjects is asked to study a list of nonsense syllables (such as LIF) that have no meaning. A second group studies a similar list and these subjects are told to try to remember the syllables by thinking of something to give it meaning (imagine a person laughing for LAF). Later in the experiment, subjects are given a recognition test. They are presented with a long list of syllables and must indicate those which were on the original list that they studied. The psychologist records the number of items recognized. For the data below, determine if the treatments are significantly different. Use the Mann-Whitney test and $\alpha = .05$.

Sample A Low Meaning	Sample B High Meaning
14	25
6	23
9	19
27	29
16	30
22	24
7	21

6. In general, a large value for the Wilcoxon T statistic indicates that there is a real difference between the treatments being compared. (True or False)

7. Rank the following difference scores and find the Wilcoxon T for this sample.

    Difference Scores: -8, 2, -10, -4, 7, -13, -17, -9

8. Briefly explain the two methods for handling difference scores of zero for the Wilcoxon T.

9. A psychologist would like to assess the effect of peer group support on weight reduction. A group of 10 people meets weekly to discuss weight loss and provide emotional and motivational support for one another. After six weeks, the psychologist records their weights to get a preliminary assessment of the effectiveness of the program. Use the Wilcoxon test to determine if a significant change has occurred after just six weeks using $\alpha = .05$. The weights before the experiment and after six weeks of meetings are as follows:

Subject	Before	After
A	201	195
B	158	150
C	151	141
D	150	143
E	171	172
F	146	149
G	162	171
H	147	142
I	145	134
J	150	138

10. The Spearman correlation will always be a positive value between zero and one. (True or False)

11. Compute the Spearman correlation for each of the following sets of data. (Note that you will need to rank order the X and Y values for the data in Set 2.)

Set 1		Set 2	
X and Y measured on ordinal scales		X and Y measured on interval scales	
X	Y	X	Y
2	5	1	5
4	1	5	2
3	2	6	9
1	4	15	20
5	3	8	4

=================

ANSWERS TO SELF-TEST

=================

1. True

2.

Scores:	3	8	8	10	14	14	14	27	35	100
Ranks:	1	2.5	2.5	4	6	6	6	8	9	10

3. False. A value of U = 0 indicates the maximum possible difference between the two treatments.

4.   The calculation of the points for sample B is as follows:

Rank	Sample	Points for B
1	A	
2	A	
3	B	---------- 4
4	A	
5	B	---------- 3
6	A	
7	A	
8	B	---------- 1
9	B	---------- 1
10	A	

Thus, sample B has a total of 9 points.   Sample A has 15 points.

5.   For sample A, U = 7, and for sample B, U = 42.   The Mann-Whitney U is 7.   With $n_A = n_B = 7$, the two-tailed critical value is 8. Reject the null hypothesis and conclude that meaningfulness does affect memory.

6.   False.   The smaller the value of the Wilcoxon T, the greater the difference between the two treatments.

7.   a.   When the difference scores are ranked in order of magnitude, it is clear that the positive values have the smaller sum of ranks.

Difference	Rank
2	1
-4	2
7	3
-8	4
-9	5
-10	6
-13	7
-17	8

The positive differences have ranks of 1 and 3, so T = 1 + 3 = 4

8.   There are two methods of dealing with difference scores of zero in a Wilcoxon test. First, you can discard the zeros and reduce the sample size. This method ignores the fact that zero differences tend to support the null hypothesis. Because it throws out data that support H_o, the practice of discarding zeros can increase the chances that you will reject the null hypothesis and increase the risk of a Type I error. The second method involves dividing the zero differences equally between the positive and negative values and ranking the zeros along with the other scores.

9.   The null hypothesis states that the weight reduction program has no systematic effect on weight. For these data the positive differences have ranks of 1, 2, and 7. The Wilcoxon T = 10.   This value is not in the critical region for n = 10, so we fail to reject the null hypothesis.

10.   False. The value of the Spearman correlation ranges from -1.00 to +1.00.

11.   For data set 1, the Spearman correlation is $r_s = -0.60$. After ranking the scores in data set 2, the Spearman correlation is $r_s = +0.50$.